HATS on HEADS

HATS on HEADS
The Art of Creative Millinery

Mildred Anlezark

Kangaroo Press

Cover: Hanna Kasschmieder wearing a Suzanne Wilks Moroccan natural straw, brim lined with cotton floral fabric

Editor: Lois Easton Graham
Photographer: Suzanne Wilks
Hats in photographs by: Lois Easton Graham, Hanna Kaschmieder and Suzanne Wilks
Cover design by Darian Causby

Reprinted 1991
This revised edition published in 1990
by Kangaroo Press Pty Ltd
3 Whitehall Road (P.O. Box 75) Kenthurst NSW 2156
Typeset by G.T. Setters Pty Limited
Printed in Singapore through Global Com Pte Ltd

ISBN 0 86417 303 2

Contents

Introduction

This book is compiled to teach the principles of construction of basic shapes of hats which have evolved over the centuries. These remain the same but the effects achieved change as fashions vary. Fashions are created by mixing or matching the crowns and brims and decreasing or increasing their size, shape, line, and direction, and combining these in such a way as to create harmony, contrast, repetition, radiation, gradation or alternation.

Colour and texture play an important part and these can also be combined in an interesting manner according to the taste of the designer.

It is essential to make an apparel plan to which the following should contribute: analysis of the figure, facial features, skin and hair colouring, and social activities.

The woman who is short and stout, with a short neck, needs a broad crown that sits high on the head. This figure type must avoid close fitting toques; a vertical trim and a drooped brim will add height.

Sometimes a woman with small facial features and a large figure needs a tip-tilted brim or crown, that is, a hat worn at a rakish angle, remembering always to balance the crown with the figure, not the face.

A very tall thin woman requires a crown that is not too tall and a brim that is not too drooped. A horizontal trim will minimise the height.

Balance must be obtained by the careful selection of a crown for the hat. The brim is not as important. Pay special attention to the shape of the head and the length of the neck. An odd-shaped head can be camouflaged by a crown that balances with the body. The hat must fit comfortably on the head. The main point to remember is to balance the crown with the general figure proportion. For example a small figure type would look ridiculous in a large crown and vice versa.

Facial features are important and the woman with well proportioned features and a long slim neck can wear a hat straight on the head. A woman with a large nose, that is out of proportion with the other features, can make it inconspicuous by wearing a brim that runs parallel to it. If the eyes are a dominant feature, a hat of the same colour will enhance them. Make sure the colour of the hat highlights the skin and hair colouring. Hair must be styled in the current fashion to gain the desired effect. A woman with a youthful or carefully made up face can wear a breton, or upturned brim.

Each era of fashion has a trend or look, therefore costume and accessories must be co-ordinated to gain a well dressed appearance. Don't consider last year's fashion, look to next year. The hat should complement the personality and the occasion for which it is worn.

Always try a hat on while standing; walk to and fro in front of a full length mirror if possible wearing the chosen costume and accessories. The whole outline must be considered, not just the head and shoulders as is usual. Lay the costume and accessories on the bed, and mix and match them, keeping in mind the colour principles.

Care of the hat

A hat must be well cared for. Put it away carefully. Make sure that feathers or flowers are flat, that veiling is folded back, and bows are padded with tissue paper. Unless there is sufficient room for the hats to be flat, rest them on their crowns, assuming of course there are no trimmings to spoil.

Materials

Interlinings

Linen canvas: This is suitable for small stitched brims, and crowns; used also for moulded crowns, blocked by wetting, and suitable for very light fabrics.

Dutch canvas: Is much heavier and more pliable than linen canvas. Suitable as a foundation for heavier fabrics, and as an alternative to cap net.

Vilene: Heavyweight vilene is suitable for large stitched brims; and is used doubled, when it is used doubled on brims, wire may be omitted; use singly for crowns. It is also used as a support for fur.

Iron-on-vilene: Used double on the brim, it is suitable for washable hats.

Nylonised cotton: Excellent for stitched hats with wide brims.

Stiffened cotton: Interlining for children's washable bonnets.

Flannelette: Suitable for berets, as it gives a soft effect.

Handicraft felt: For stitched section hats, and berets. It gives a padded effect. Also effective used with organza.

Foam plastic: This can be bought to various specifications. It is excellent used in conjunction with willow. Wadding or batting is also used for padding crowns.

Crinoline: A transparent resilient fabric, and is suitable for lightweight fabrics, e.g. nylon, organdie.

Cap net: Also known as Dior net, or Paris net. This net is blocked to shape and is ideal for lightweight hats of petals, and a foundation for lace or lightweight fabrics.

Net: This can also be used as an interlining for lightweight fabrics, and as a lining for straws and lightweight hats.

Willow: Made from hemp, a grass fibre, it is mainly imported from Hong Kong, and is made in sheets, 24'' × 32'' (61 × 81 cm). The right side has a cotton covering, and the wrong side is the grass. Willow is made pliable with the use of steam or a dampened sponge. The pliability comes from the bias of the material. Care must be taken not to wet the willow too much as the cotton covering will lift from the grass. The only time the willow is thoroughly wet is when a brim is to be moulded with a hot iron, this is also the only time the wrong side of the willow is used, otherwise the cotton covering will lift.

Willow is suitable foundation for heavyweight fabrics, furs, stitched fabrics, and when a more tailored type of hat is wanted.

Leno or marli: This is a less expensive base and is quite firm. Dip in water and allow to become limp; place over block and pull down. (See page 100). Brims cut to pattern should not be dampened. Buckram is also used but not recommended.

Covering fabrics

May be satin, silk, cotton, velvet or wool. Special millinery fabrics are obtainable but most dress fabrics are suitable for the manufacture of hats. Furs real and imitation, leather and plastic are all suitable materials from which to make hats. Also straw and felt hoods and capelines may be purchased and shaped as desired. Straw braid and crinoline may be purchased in several metre lengths which is stitched to form a shape. Fine Shapewell cut on the bias, then folded in the centre, is cheaper and better.

Linings: Are usually silk, soft synthetics, or cotton net, according to the type of hat to be lined. White is the better colour to use unless the hat is transparent. Every hat should be finished with a moulded ribbon headband; this is usually 1'' (2.5 mm) wide and is purchased as grosgrain or petersham, and this too is usually in white.

Trimmings: The trimmings for a hat are far too many to list, as they range from painted curtain rings tied with felt, through to leather, patent leather, to beads, feathers and a host of ribbons and fabrics.

Stiffening solutions: Now only one strength called Felt Size and Straw Stiffener.

Panama stiffener: Mix 2 oz (60 ml) of selley's Aquadhere with 50 oz (150 ml) lukewarm water. Mix well, apply with damp cloth and allow to dry.

Adhesive: Used when a fabric is required to be moulded to a curve in willow, and is used when stitches cannot be used effectively.

Wires: Millinery wire is made in black or white, and is purchased by the coil. It ranges in gauge from thick heavily padded satin wire, to silk covered, and very fine wire named ribbon. Electricians' fuse wire is used for threaded beads for bridal wear. Although the wires may only be purchased in black or white, the white wire may be coloured with water colour pencils or aniline dye.

Needles: Needles used in millinery are called "straw", they are a long needle (sizes 7 & 8). For machine stitched fabric hats No. 11 needles are best.

Thread: For willow, a glace thread No. 24 is suitable. For felt No. 40 sylko in a tone to match the felt. For stitched fabric hats, No. 50 supershene cotton is best. Stranded cotton, Broder cotton, or Raffia is used to stitch straw braid.

Millinery Terminology

Calico	or	muslin
Cross	or	bias
Cotton	or	thread
Drawing pins	or	tacks
Tack	or	baste
Tip	or	lid
Turnings	or	seam allowance
Moire	or	water wave (silk)
Model hat	means	one only creation
Semi-model	means	a limited number
Ready to wear	means	unlimited number

(Note: The word 'model' is used very loosely today)

Measurements

1 inch	= 2.5 centimetres (approx.)
12 inches	= 30 centimetres (approx.)
1 yard	= 0.91 metres (approx.)
39.37 inches (approx.)	= 1 metre

Head sizes

Inches	English	Can/USA	Metric
20	6⅜	6½	51 cm
20½	6½	6⅝	52 cm
21	6⅝	6¾	53 cm
21½	6¾	6⅞	55 cm
22	6⅞	7	56 cm
22½	7	7⅛	57 cm
23	7⅛	7¼	58 cm
23½	7¼	7⅜	59 cm
24	7⅜	7½	61 cm
24½	7½	7⅝	62 cm
25	7⅝	7¾	63 cm
25½	7¾	7⅞	65 cm
26	7⅞	8	66 cm

Children's head sizes

18½″ - 20½″ (47 - 52 cm)	=	1 - 4 years
19½″ (49.5 cm)	=	small
20½″ (52 cm)	=	medium
21½ (54.5 cm)	=	large

Measuring

The head fitting measurement is taken firmly around the forehead and over the occipital prominence at the back of the head. This will be referred to as the nape. To this amount add one to two inches (2.5 to 5 cm) according to the type of material used, for example hats made of fabric by the metre take up more room than felt.

Measure over the top of the head from the tip of one ear to the tip of the other. From the forehead at the hairline, to the nape of the neck.

When hats are worn straight on the head take measurements with a piece of ribbon; try on and adjust for comfort. Use this ribbon for the head band inside the hat and you cannot then fail to get the correct size.

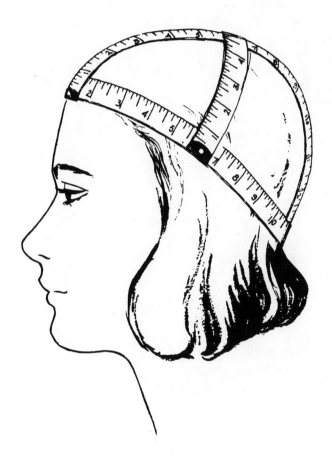

Stitches

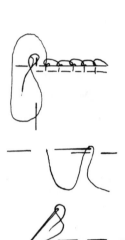

Buttonhole stitch used to attach wire to crowns and brims.

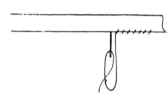

Backstitch used where strength is required.

Tacking used to hold two pieces of material temporarily.

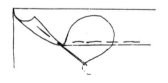

Straight hemming for felt brim edges and applying crowns to brims.

Slip stitch an invisible stitch for brim edge finishes, applying lining.

Stab stitch is used for making a join in willow.

Overcasting to stop a raw edge from fraying.

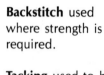

Threadline to outline a pattern.

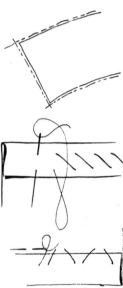

Diagonal basting used to attach one fabric to another.

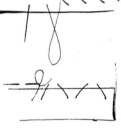

Catch stitch used for lightness e.g. to catch a fold in a crown.

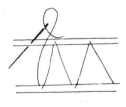

Lacing stitch to secure two edges of fabric together.

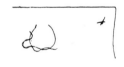

Tie stitch for attaching trimmings e.g. flowers, feathers.

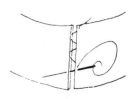

Darning to make a join in felt.

Felt Hoods and Capelines

Felts are made in two shapes:

1. THE HOOD which is a cone shape, is suitable for small head-hugging and draped toques, or small brimmed hats.
2. THE CAPELINE is much larger than the hood and it allows for a large brimmed hat.

Hoods and capelines are made from wool or fur. The wool is the cheaper variety of hood and capeline.

Fur felt hoods and capelines are made from the fur of the rabbit, hare, muskrat, nutria and beaver.

The manufacture of these hoods undergoes four processes i.e. carroting, blowing, forming, hardening. This is called the wet side of the industry. Furs are washed when necessary with strong whale oil soap and water to remove encrusted dirt. Then they are treated with nitrate of mercury which opens out the small barbs that each fur fibre is covered with. This process is known as carroting.

The skins are then fed into a machine, which cuts the hide to shreds and blows the fur onto an endless belt. The fur is graded into different qualities, and is then fed into a machine which has thousands of steel pickers. These pickers separate the down from the kemp of the fibre. This process is known as blowing.

Forming is done by feeding the down onto a perforated cone, it is then wrapped with flannel and covered with another metal cone. This is then immersed in hot water.

For the hardening process the formed hood is lifted from the metal cone, and is subjected to heat, moisture, pressure and motion, until the fibres become firmly interlocked. These processes are carried out until enough shrinkage occurs. Then the hood is treated with a solution of shellac and methylated spirit. It is then placed in a kiln, the heat welds the fibres together so closely they cannot be separated in later operations.

In the dry side of the industry when the milliner is ready to block the hood or capeline to its ultimate shape, the steam used softens the shellac allowing the hood to become pliable, and so it is shaped as required. It is then left to dry thoroughly on the wooden block.

Hood

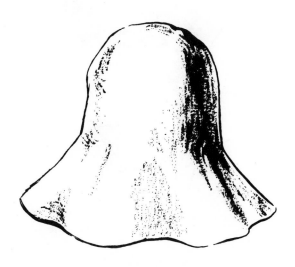

Capeline

To Block a Felt Hood or Capeline

1. Decide on the shape required.
2. Select a block or blocks to or nearest to the shape required, and to the headfitting plus ½'' (12 mm) on the collar and one inch on the crown block. If the hat is to be blocked all in one, one half inch on the headfitting will suffice.

Sometimes to obtain a specific shape it may be necessary to use more than one block in the process. For example the felt may need stretching on a beret block to obtain enough material for folds. Care must be taken not to tear the felt, especially if it is a remodel, as the felt may be thin in places. If the felt is held to the light weak spots (if any) will show.

Make sure that the block is clean, it may be covered with butter muslin or cellophane to avoid soiling, especially if the hood is immersed in water sometimes the dye runs and soils the wooden block. Tissue paper and Glad-Wrap can also be used.

Steam

Hold the hood over the spout of the steamer and fill the inside of the hood with steam. When the hood has become pliable and soft, quickly place it over the block (which is ½'' (12 mm) larger than the head fitting), and working quickly, grasp the edge of the hood with the forefingers and thumbs, pull the hood down, and smooth out any air bubbles at the top with the tips of the fingers. The hood can be dampened well on the inside rubbed around evenly with a small cotton cloth. Roll up in a clean tea-towel for a couple of hours—the hood will then become soft and very pliable. A kettle with a small spout used on a stove, or an electric kettle with a similar spout, which boils without cutting off are good substitutes for the Jiffy. Electric jugs are not suitable.

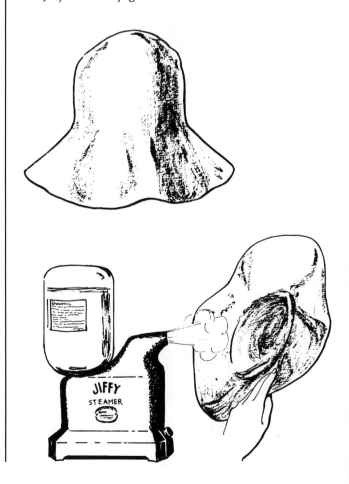

Select a style, keeping in mind the elements of design and their principles.

It will be noted that some felts made of wool will harden quickly as the steam dissipates from the hood, then it may be necessary to dip the hood in warm water and mould over the block instead of using steam. Hoods made from fur such as Melusine which is light in texture will mould easily, whilst the heavy textured Velour requires more time and patience.

Smooth the felt to the configuration of the block, some felts will be easier than others. Melusine is quite pliable but velour is more difficult. If folds are required in the crown, then these are moulded in position with the fingers. If a hat is to be copied, then the picture should be in front of the worker.
    Allow the felt to dry.

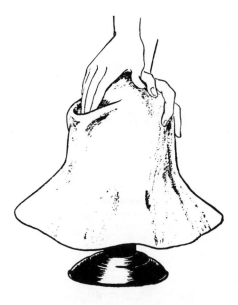

unwanted wrinkles. A kettle with a small spout is good—you need a dry steam. Do not use a jug.

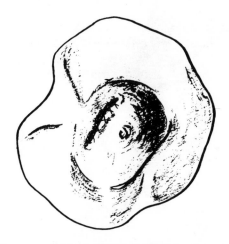

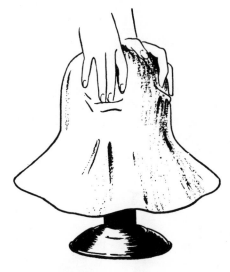

    Place an elastic band at the depth of the head fitting. **N.B.** The stitching of the folds may be left until the crown is thoroughly dry and is cut away from the brim.

When dry enough to handle, the fold is sewn in position with a catch stitch or several bar stitches. Place the capeline back on the block and steam to remove any

First mark centre front of crown and brim with a coloured thread, and tie off. Place berry pins in the elastic band to hold it in position. Mark with tailor's chalk. Cut the brim away from the crown with a razor blade.

If the design requires the brim all in one with the crown, then the felt is smoothed over a brim block—which is placed in position under the crown block—and berry pins are placed in the brim edge.

Allow the felt to dry thoroughly, this is important because the felt will go out of shape if it is not dry. Stiffen the inside with felt size. Handle it carefully and sit it back on the block to dry.

Select a brim block to the style required, and a collar that is ½'' (12 mm) larger than the head fitting.

Place the felt on the block, allowing ½'' (13 mm) to sit up around the collar. If the felt is too large and it won't shrink with steaming, a join will have to be made in the back or a pleat may be made at the side. Steam the felt and smooth away any wrinkles.

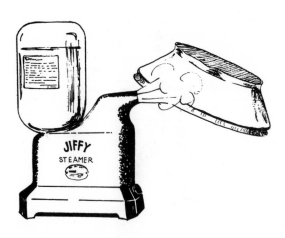

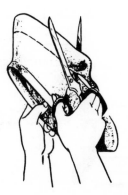

Cut away surplus felt, allowing ¼'' (6 mm) for a hem if required.

Place an elastic band around the collar. Drawing pins can be placed in the collar as it will be covered with the crown. Place berry pins at the brim edge. Allow the brim to dry thoroughly. Mark for the depth of the crown from the base of the block using tailor's chalk.

Take the spring out of a coiled wire by stroking with the forefinger and thumb.

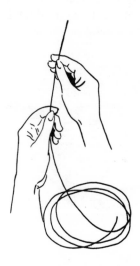

Place the wire at the centre back. Allow a good overlap of wire for the join. Fold the felt over the wire and hem, using small straight hemming stitches. For Bretons and shaped brims it is better to buttonhole the wire on the turning line, and then make a hem of any width.

Steam the hem, rolling it between fingers to obscure the stitches.

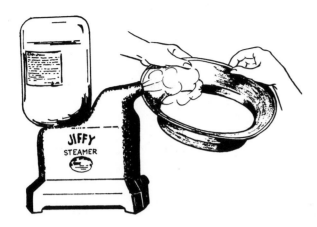

Stiffen the inside of the brim with felt size and allow to dry thoroughly. Place the crown over the brim. This may be hemmed with small stitches, or if the stitches are to be covered then back stitches will suffice.

The crown being stitched to the brim.

Apply the trimming with the minimum amount of stitching.

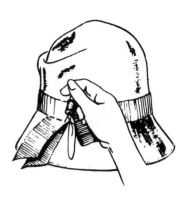

Wet ¾ yard (69 cm) of 1'' (25 mm) wide grosgrain ribbon. Mould it to an arc with a hot iron.

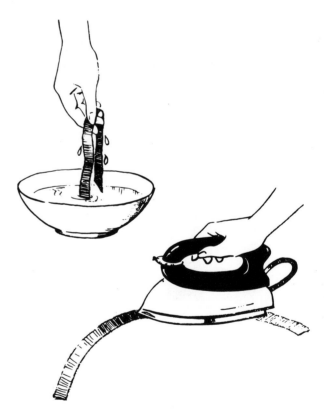

With the large arc of the ribbon to the base of the crown, and the shiny or ironed side to the felt, start at the centre back with ½'' (13 mm) extending for a seam, fit the ribbon to the head fitting. Stitch an open seam on the wrong side of the ribbon with a back stitch. Cut away surplus ribbon. Stitch the ribbon to the head fitting using a long stitch (¼'' – ⅜'' or 6-9 mm) on the underside of the ribbon and a tiny stitch on the right side, taking the needle back and forth almost in the same hole and between the grooves in the ribbon. This stitch can go through to the outside if it is going to be covered with a trim. The ribbon head band may be applied to the brim before the crown is attached.

Give the felt a final light steaming, brushing in a circular motion to raise the nap.

If the crown has been extended with an insert of willow, then a sixteen pleat lining is required.

If an elastic is required to hold the hat on the head, then this is attached to either side of the collar under the ribbon, with a few knots in the elastic, and a few stitches to hold it in position. Place elastic 4½'' (115 mm) from centre front. For length, measure elastic from 4½'' (115 mm) point around back to other point. This is usually the correct length. Make elastic adjustable by stitching closely, but not through the elastic.

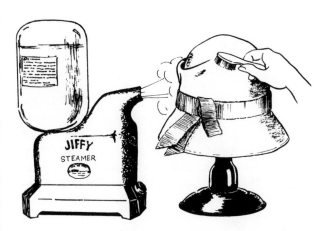

To prepare a felt hat for remodelling

Remove all trimmings and wire. If the hat has any stitching remove this also. Very often the crown and brim are in two pieces.

If the felt is soiled then it may be washed in soapy water. Gently dunk it in and out of the water. Rub soap (Sunlight or Sard) on any extra dirty spots. Then rinse in warm water. Gently squeeze out surplus water.

Wash the felt on the day required and place it in a plastic bag. If the felt must be washed earlier then it may be placed over an upturned basin or saucepan until required for steaming.

Some alternative methods of brim finishes

1. Instead of hemming a wire to the brim edge, the wire may be eliminated, the edge cut without turnings, and several rows of machine stitching may be worked around the edge.

The cut edge of the felt to be finely sandpapered to smooth the edge.
2. The wire may be closely satin stitched to the cut brim edge with matching, stranded embroidery thread.
3. A wire is buttonholed to the edge of the cut felt and covered with a shaped grosgrain ribbon, folded in halves and stab-stitched diagonally in the grooves of the ribbon, from the right to the wrong side, with an invisible stitch attaching both edges simultaneously.
4. Narrow or wide bias folds of bias fabric may be used to trim the wired edge.
5. Providing the brim is not too large and the appropriate felt is used, it may be stiffened with extra felt size and the wire eliminated and the edge sandpapered.
If the brim is turned up in front and down at the back and a wired hem used, then the wire will require to be reversed where the brim starts to curve. It is necessary to make a nick in the quarter inch extension to enable the wire and hem to be reversed.

To make a join in felt, place the cut edge of the felt together and weave with a fine darning stitch, working on the right side with matching thread.

Sixteen Pleat Lining

Fabric required is a ½ yd (46 cm) of soft taffeta, white for preference.

Draw a circle with 2'' (5 cm) radius, and make this oval, in shape, by adding a ¼'' (6 mm) to the centre front and subtracting ¼'' (6 mm) from the side. Fold the paper in four and cut out. This ensures a balanced oval. Trace an extra oval on paper, with a seam allowance, this is stitched in with the fabric to ensure perfection. It can be torn away later.

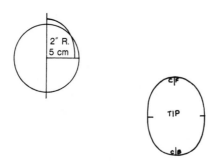

Now fold the fabric, on the bias. To do this take hold of one corner and fold one edge at right angles to the other. Cut out a bias strip of fabric, to the length of the head fitting measure plus seam allowance, and width the depth of the crown plus seam allowance. Mark this off in sixteen sections.

Cut an oval C.F. on the straight grain in the fabric allowing ½'' (13 mm) seam.

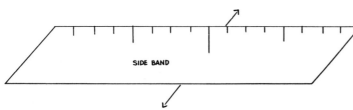

Threadline round the patterns, define the corners. Mark the bias head band and the tip in four with a thread.

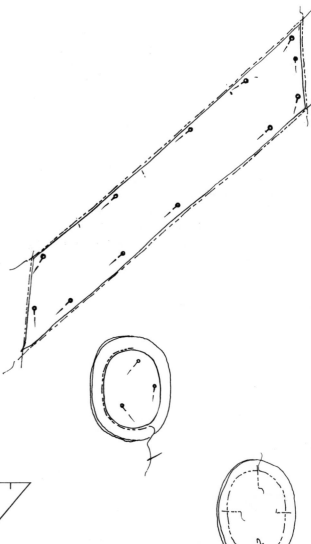

20

Pin, tack and machine the centre back seam. Cut away surplus fabric to make the seam ½'' (13 mm). Press the seam open.

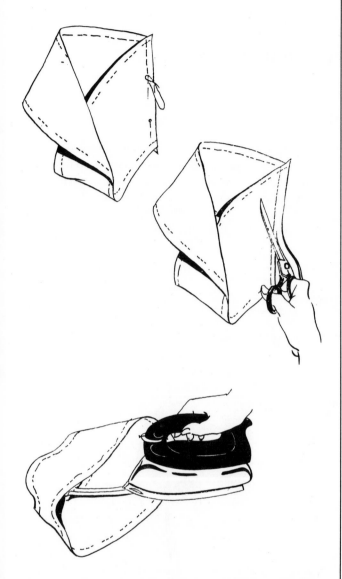

Machine sew the seam, following the pencilled line on the paper. Tear away the paper.

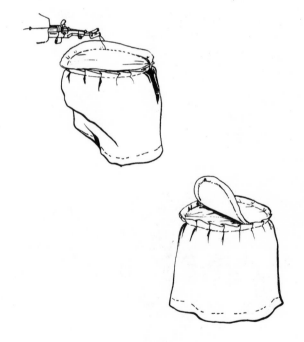

The true centre back of the seam is regarded as halfway along the diagonal seam. Pleat the marked off section to form sixteen pleats. Pin the tip with the paper attached to the side band matching the four marked sections. Tack, to hold in position.

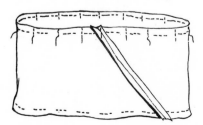

Brim Block Construction from Radii

Brim blocks may be made from heavy cardboard (Russel board) by drawing a series of circles with the use of the tape measure and a pencil. The tape measure must be of the type with a hole in one end.

The first circle is drawn at 4'' (10 cm), therefore insert a drawing pin at 4⅜'' (11 cm) on the tape measure; this ⅜'' (1 cm) allowance is because the hole in the tape measure is ⅜'' (1 cm) in from the edge. Draw a complete circle. These brims are 2'' (5 cm) wide so insert the drawing pin at 6⅜'' (16.2 cm) on the tape measure and draw another circle. A series of these circles are made by adding 2'' (5 cm) each time, therefore, making a larger circle each time until 12'' (30.5 cm) is reached.

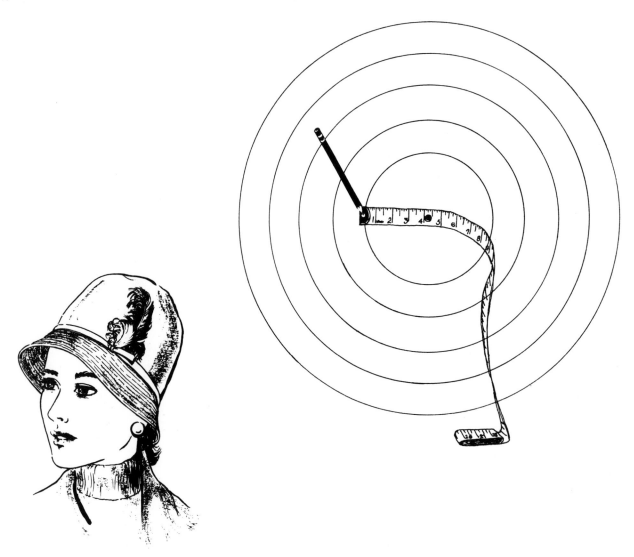

Draw a line from the central point where the drawing pin was inserted through all the circles and at any desirable point. This line represents one centre back line of each brim. To find the other centre back line, measure around each circle (excepting the final one) with a tape measure carefully following the curve until the headfitting is reached, not forgetting to add at least one inch to this measure for take up in material.

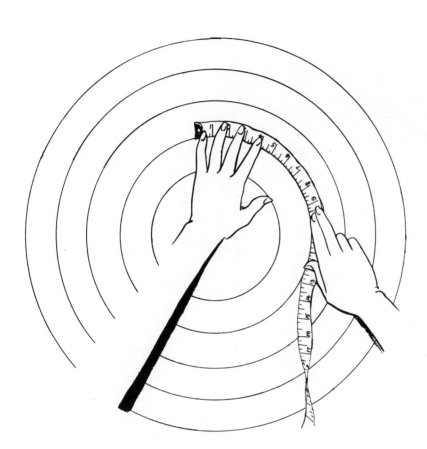

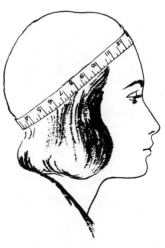

The brim patterns are then cut out and are used to mould canvas, cap net, willow, felt or straw.

It will be noticed that the first or centre circle with the small radius stands out from the forehead straighter than the longer one, the latter being close fitting or 'cloche'. Therefore the longer the radius the more the droop.

If the brims are required to be narrower at the back then this amount (say half an inch; 12 mm) may be marked on the board and a new curve made.

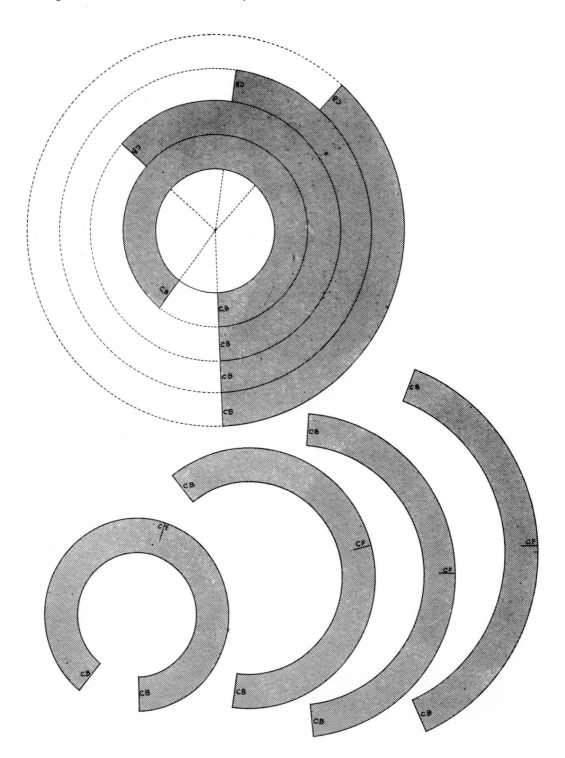

Construction of Brim from Radii

Fold ¾ yard (69 cm) of linen canvas on the true bias, take hold of one corner and fold it at right angles; cut along the entire length of the fold. Measure out a 6'' (15 cm) wide strip on the longest length, and cut this off.

Wet the bias strip of canvas (sopping wet) and mould it around the selected Russel-board brim block. Encase the brim block with the wet canvas, pulling on the bias of the canvas at the headfitting. Place berry pins along the headfitting and centre backs, making sure that the canvas is fitting smoothly and allow to dry.

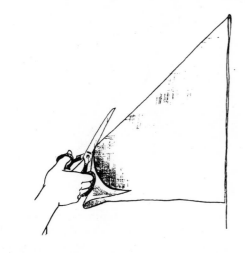

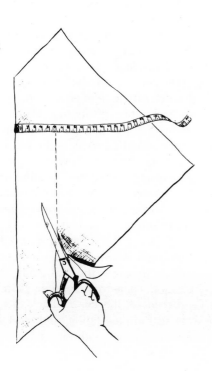

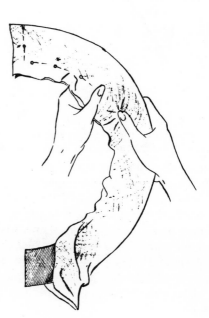

When the canvas is completely dry, it may need ironing to remove any bubbles. Pencil around the headfitting and centre backs on both sides. Carefully remove the canvas from the brim block and sew the back seam. Carefully press open the seam, and cut away surplus canvas to ½'' (13 mm).

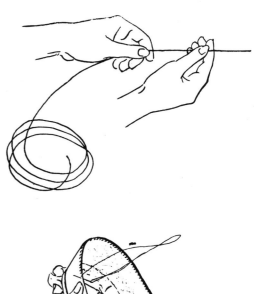

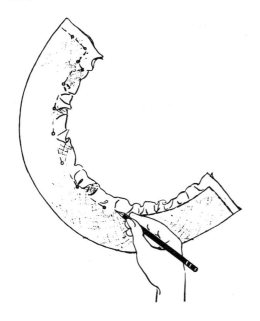

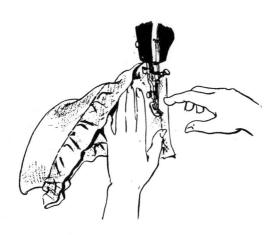

Take the spring out of a section of millinery wire, by stroking it with the forefinger and thumb, this makes the coil larger and easier to handle. Cut off the approximate amount of wire required plus a good two inches for overlap. This large overlap is required otherwise the wire would poke through the canvas. If the whole coil of wire is left attached whilst sewing it to the brim, the wire would drag and distort the brim shape. Make sure the wire is cut cleanly. Place this length of wire in the fold of the canvas and holding it in position with the left hand, button-hole stitch on the outside, starting 1'' (25 mm) from the centre back. Finish with the overlaps as mentioned.

Cut a length of ½'' (13 mm) tape, the headfitting plus 1'' (25 mm) plus 1'' for overlap, join this to make a circle. Place this tape around the headfitting of the canvas just touching the pencil line, this is called the collar. Stab-stitch this tape to the collar.

Cut a length of fabric, to cover the canvas, in the same manner as described for cutting the canvas strip, the same width and length. Place this fabric face down with ½'' (13 mm) extending at the centre back and on the canvas. Pin the centre of the fabric on the brim edge, with berry pins, placing the pins in a vertical position. Before each pin is placed, stretch the centre of the fabric. Stretching the fabric along the centre like this, reduces the amount of fullness on the cut edges and so allows for a snug fitting, wrinkle free covering. When the pinning and fitting is completed, mark with a berry pin centre back or seamline of the fabric. Remove the fabric from the brim and position the seam so as to obtain a bias join (straight grain). If the fabric is held up it will be found to be a continuous circle. This bias join looks and sits better on the brim than the straight join with the bias grain. The very centre of this bias join is the true centre back, and this point must be placed on the centre back of the canvas brim. Tack the seam in the fabric, and try it on the brim to see if it fits smoothly, without tightness or looseness.

When satisfied with the fit, machine-stitch the seam, do not hand seam this as it is not satisfactory. Press the seam open and cut seam allowance back ½'' (13 mm). Place the fabric back on the brim, right side up and place pins in the collar in a vertical position.

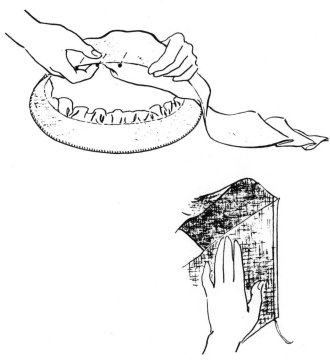

Commence to sew (see notes on machine sewing) starting at the centre back, and with the zipper foot attached to the machine, complete one row of machine stitching, finishing opposite to the first stitch made.

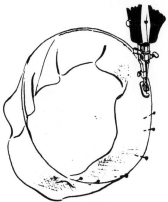

Replace the zipper foot with the ordinary foot, allowing the needle to remain in the fabric. Sew in continuous circles until the collar is reached, using the small foot as a guide to keep the stitching an even width apart all around, meanwhile stretching at the headfitting to reduce fullness, and keeping an eye on the underside for wrinkles. Remove the berry pins as practicable. Tie the stitches at beginning and end. The brim is now ready to attach to a felt crown, or fabric crown.

To assemble

Felt crown

Place felt crown over collar of brim, and stitch with a backstitch on the right side; usually this hat has a trimming around the crown, therefore, the stitching would be covered.

Fabric crown

The brim is placed upside down on the crown, with the headfitting of the crown to the collar of the brim; tack and machine stitch on the wrong side.

Cut away surplus fabric from collar.

Trim the hat in harmony with the style. The trimming is very lightly attached. If it is a band of ribbon or fabric, then it is only sewn at the join. If feathers, leaves or flowers are used then these are attached with a tie stitch. These stitches to be invisible.

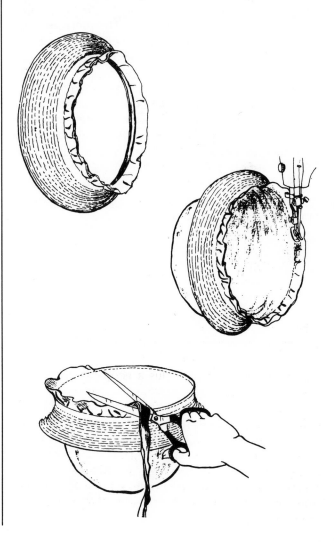

Crown Pattern Construction from Radii

The longer the radius the straighter the sides of the crown, for example, a 15'' (38 cm) radius gives a plant pot shape whereas a 36'' (91.5 cm) radius allows for a Pill Box, with straight sides. (A bias strip.)

A variety of crown shapes may be made from radii—they may be deep and draped into folds, or folded to one side, or left smooth.

Rule a line down the centre of the paper, this is the centre front, and start by making a radius of 15'' (38 cm), making a ⅜'' (1 cm) allowance for the hole in the tape measure, to the right side of the centre front line. This curve or arc is measured for half the headfitting not forgetting to add allowance to the headfitting for the take-up in material.

Decide upon the height of the crown required and take this amount away from the radius inserting the drawing pin in the same mark just made and make another arc. A straight line is ruled from the headfitting mark, through the second arc. This line is the centre back line. This defines the shape of the crown.

The draft is folded in half on the centre front line and cut along the headfitting line, the centre back line, and along what is called the area edge.

To find the radius for the 'tip', measure the area edge, and minus one inch, divide by six.

Trace out this pattern instruction.

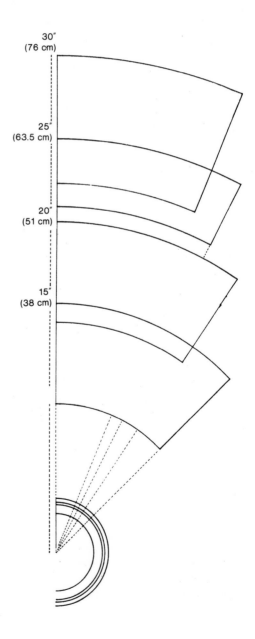

Brim Pattern Construction from Radii Variation

A wider brim may be constructed from the Russel board blocks made in a previous lesson. Decide the droop required, 4'' (10 cm) droop has a slight droop and a 6'' (15 cm) a little more and so on. If the brim block is placed against the forehead the type of droop required will soon become familiar. The centre front and sides must be marked.

Place the Russel board block of the selected droop, onto the drawing paper and outline the headline, centre backs, and brim area with a pencil. Mark centre front and sides. This brim pattern may now be enlarged or reduced in width by measuring out from the headfitting, for example the centre front may be taken to 3½'' (9 cm), the sides to 3'' (7.6 cm), and the back 1½'' (38 mm). These marks just made are then joined with a curved pencilled line to form a different shaped brim with the droop selected. It is a good idea to curve only half of the brim then the pattern may be folded down the centre and the double piece is cut out with an equal curve either side. Of course if the brim is required to have unequal sides then the whole brim must be curved freehand. This brim pattern may be cut and spread in one place to obtain a flute or cut and darted to obtain more droop in one or more places.

When a brim is wider than 2'' (5 cm), then two pieces of fabric must be cut, this brim has a seam on the edge. A bias strip of fabric, in most cases, will not stretch effectively beyond a two inch brim.

A double thickness of vilene or nylonised cotton is used for interlining in this brim, and as the brim is to be stitched then the wire usually used on the brim edge may be omitted.

Cut two brims in interlining, if there is a grain in the fabric then the centre front is placed on the bias, vilene has no grain. Allow half an inch seam allowance. Mark around the patterns in pencil, making sure to define the corners, and mark the centre front.

Place these two interlinings onto the wrong side of fabric with the centre front on the bias. Cut out leaving half an inch seam allowance. Tack around the pencilled lines, catching together the fabric and interlining. (Caution—if white or transparent fabric is used, pencil must not be used.)

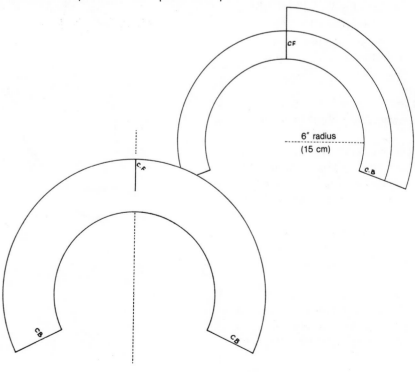

6'' radius
(15 cm)

Construction of Simple Stitched Hat from Radii Patterns

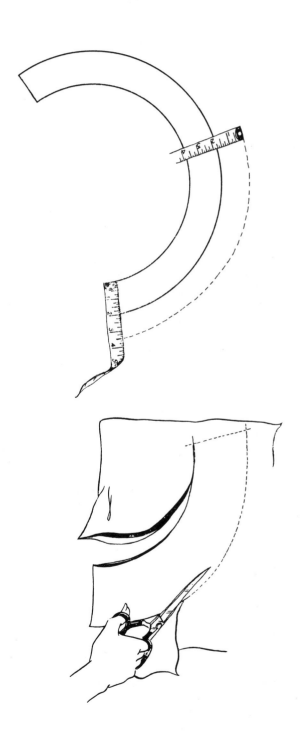

Fabric Required

1 yard (91.5 cm) of 36'' (91.5 cm) millinery or suitable dress fabric, or ¾ yard (69 cm) of 54'' (1.37 m) fabric.
1 yard (91.5 cm) vilene or nylonised cotton for interlining.
½ yard (46 cm) soft taffeta (white for preference).
¾ yard (69 cm) 1'' (25 mm) grosgrain white ribbon.
No. 50 supershene cotton to tone or contrast with the main fabric.
Contrasting thread (not red) for threadlining.
White thread for lining fabric and ribbon head-band.

This hat is suitable for a vilene interlining; a double brim of vilene is cut, this eliminates the use of wire on the brim edge. Choose a style of hat suitable for radii construction. Select a crown from radii and a brim from the russel brim blocks.

Extend the brim block to the width required, by drawing round the outline of the russel board and measuring out from the centre front, side and back. Recurve the outline.

Trace out round the outline of half the headfitting and the new brim edge. Fold the paper in halves and cut out the pattern. If an uneven shaped brim is required, then the whole of the pattern must be shaped from the brim block.

Place the patterns on the vilene and pencil round the outline, defining the corners. Vilene has no grain, and it does not matter how the patterns are placed on this, but it is better to form the habit of placing patterns in the correct position. Cut out allowing ½'' (13 mm) for seams.

Place the interlining onto the wrong side of the fabric, placing the centre fronts of the brims on the bias, also the crown; the centre front of the tip is cut on the straight grain. Cut out round the outline of the interlining. Tack the interlining and fabric together, defining the corners.

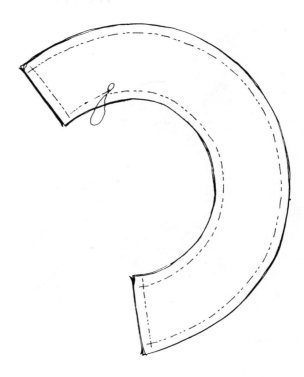

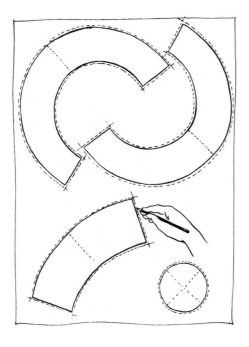

Pin, tack and machine sew the centre backs of the brims.

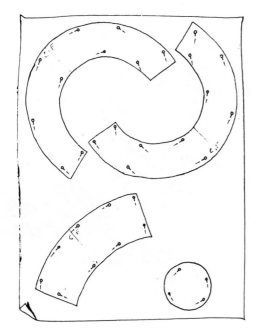

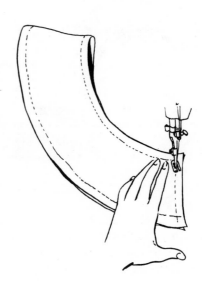

Cut the interlining back to the machine stitching and trim the seam allowance.

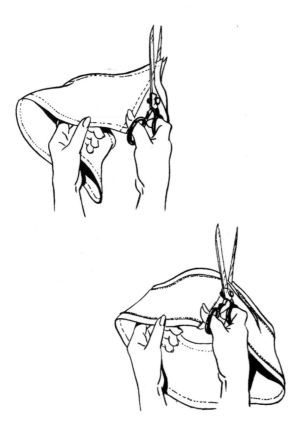

Press open the seam.

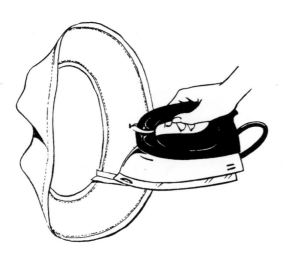

Place the brims right sides together, pin, tack and machine sew around the brim edge. Trim the interlining to the machine stitching and cut the seam to ¼'' (6 mm). Turn through to the right side.

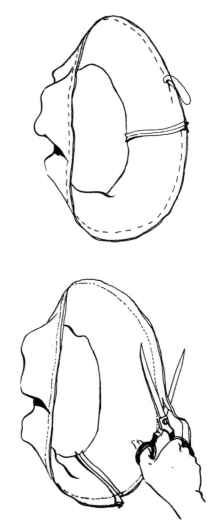

Press the brim.

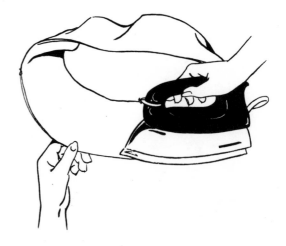

Commence to stitch, starting at the centre back at the brim edge, stitch in continuous circles, finishing at the collar. Cut into the headfitting at half inch intervals, and press the brim.

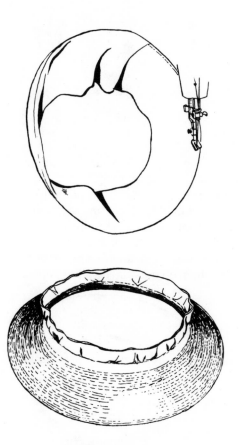

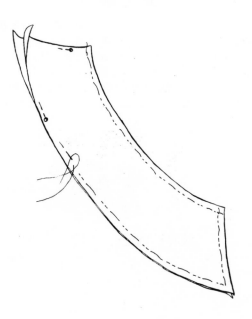

Tack the interlining to the wrong side of the crown.

The pattern for the stitching is worked out by dividing the crown and tip into sections and then drawing diagonal lines or circles or leaves into these spaces. This can be practised on the paper patterns then transferred to the interlining. Tack the main guide lines so that they will show on the right side. Threadline through to the right side, the design lines to be followed. These design lines are pencilled on the vilene first.

The centre patterns are better worked first, this stops the fabric from 'bubbling'.

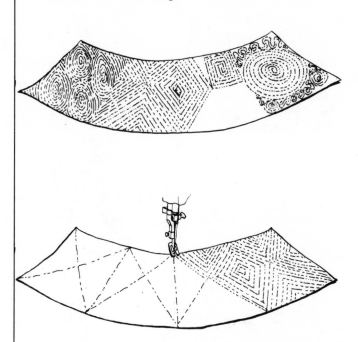

All stitching is better carried out on the right side (fabric side). Using the small side of the foot on the machine as a guide, and starting on the outside of the pattern, lower the presser foot. Place the needle in the cloth and holding the cotton to the back of the machine with the left hand, proceed to sew. Sew in continuous circles until the centre is reached, the threads are cut and pulled through to the wrong side and tied. This applies to circular designs such as leaves. If a diagonal design is decided upon then the stitching is started at the raw edge of the fabric, stitch along the diagonal line until the point is reached and leaving the needle in the cloth, lift the presser and turn the fabric, lower the presser foot and continue to sew along the triangle. Make sure that each row of stitching matches at the back.

To make up crown

Pin and tack and machine stitch the centre seam of the crown, cut away interlining to the machine stitching. Press open the seam and trim to ½'' (13 mm). Place the tip in position, matching the centre fronts, pin, tack and machine stitch. Trim surplus fabric.

If the crown is required draped, then the folds are catch-stitched in place.

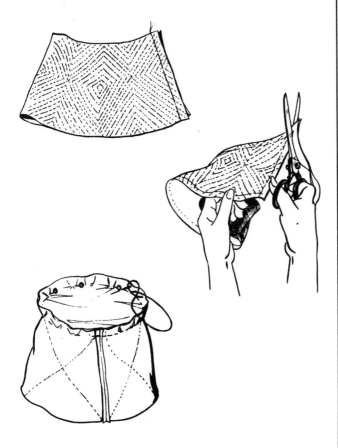

Place the right side of the brim to the right side of the crown; Pin, tack and machine sew. Trim the surplus fabric. Trim the hat at this stage.

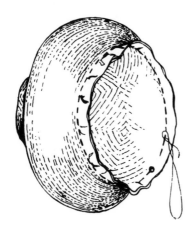

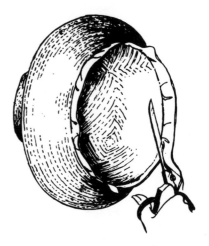

Make headlining from the same pattern as the crown, this is usually made in a soft taffeta. Machine sew the tip with paper underneath divided into four.

The headlining is placed in the crown, making sure that it fits snugly, and is not too shallow or too large. Turn under the edge of the lining at the headfitting and slipstitch this to the headfitting of the brim, taking up a machine stitch on the brim headline with each slipstitch.

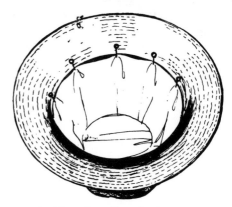

A moulded ribbon headband of grosgrain is stitched in place. A hat elastic may be attached if desired. This is placed under the ribbon, between the brim headband and the ribbon and is secured with a stitch and a knot in the elastic 4½'' (115 mm) from centre front, and the length of the elastic is the distance from that point around the back of the crown to the other point.

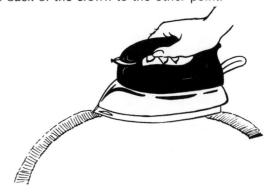

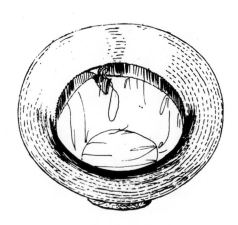

Machine sewing

Most modern domestic sewing machines built for Australian conditions are set to take fine fabrics, therefore fine cotton and needle give the best results.

No. 50 Supershene cotton and No. 11 needle, is advised to use with the automatic sewing machines now produced. On the old machines use size 14 medium, or No. 16 for heavy work.

Before commencing to sew, remove any oil or dust from the machine. Check the needle to see that it is not blunt or bent. Make sure the needle is correctly placed and threaded correctly. The last threading guide denotes whether the needle is to be threaded from the right or left side or front. This rule also applies to the placement of the needle, the flat side of the needle faces away from the last threading guide. Make sure the bobbin is evenly wound and is placed in the shuttle with the cotton against the tension. Be sure to have the bobbin thread up through the needle hole and the two threads towards the back of the machine. A turn of the balance wheel will bring the bobbin thread to the top.

Tensions are important, this means that there must be no looping of threads on either side, the stitching on either side must be even. The right side or upper is always the better machining, therefore the right side of a brim should be uppermost when stitching.

Sit in a comfortable position at the machine, in a straight backed chair for preference, directly opposite the presser foot, rest the elbows comfortably on the machine. Always hold the two threads of cotton when commencing to sew for two stitches, this avoids cotton locks. Do not drag the fabric through the machine, let the feed dog do its work. Use the balance wheel as a brake, control is important, especially when stitching circles. Use one part of the foot as a guide for straight stitching. Keep one part of the foot against the last row of stitching and watch the foot not the needle. Practise on a scrap of fabric first.

To attach the zipper foot, raise the presser foot, and the needle to its highest point. Undo the thumbscrew and remove the presser foot. Attach the zipper foot and tighten the thumbscrew with the screwdriver, this tightening is essential as the foot must be firm. The zipper foot may be adjusted from right to left by undoing the thumbscrew at the back and sliding the foot along the bar at the back, retighten the screw.

Fluted Brim

This brim is constructed with the use of a wooden collar, it is an alternative method of pattern construction. Select a collar ½'' (13 mm) larger than the headfitting.

As this brim is different either side, all of the pattern is constructed in the initial stage.

Draw a vertical line down the centre of a sheet of paper. Centre the collar on this, and pencil round the outline. If a collar is not obtainable then a heavy satin wire the length required and joined to form a circle and flattened at the sides to form an oval will suffice.

Rightangle from the centre of the collar on either side. Bisect these angles and measure from the headfitting along these lines to shape the brim. Where the brim is required to droop or curve, dart these areas. Do not make a dart larger than 1'' (25 mm). It is better to have more smaller darts than less larger ones.

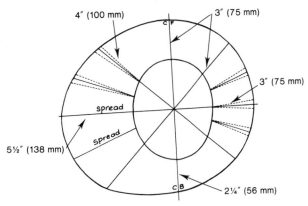

This brim because it is fluted will need to be cut and spread or cut and wedges inserted. The method used will be according to type. If the pattern overlaps at the back when it has been spread, the join instead of being at the centre back, will have to be made at a convenient distance either side of the centre back.

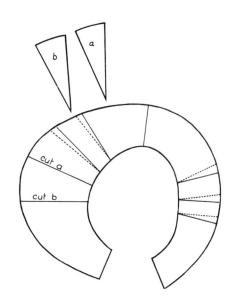

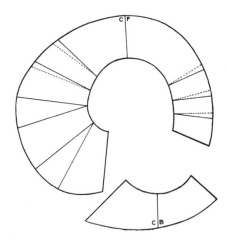

The Beret

The beret may be made in a variety of fabrics and inter-linings to suit the particular occasion, costume and season.

1. Velvet or velveteen—flannelette interlining.
2. Stitched satin—handicraft felt interlining.
3. Organza—handicraft felt interlining.
4. Organza—net interlining.
5. Fur fabric or fur—minus interlining.
6. Faile—linen canvas interlining.
7. Showerproof fabric—vilene interlining, foamrubber, or minus interlining.
8. Wool jersey—foam rubber interlining.
9. Foam rubber backed fabric.

The beret may be trimmed in many and varied ways. With a pompom, feather, hat pin, ribbon bow, grosgrain ribbon trim.

Beret pattern construction

To construct the patterns for the simple beret, two circles are drawn, one for the headfitting and one for the tip or top of the beret.

For this beret the scale for the radii is based on 3½'' (9 cm) equals 22'' (56 cm) headfitting and each subsequent ⅛'' (3 mm) equals 1'' (25 mm) of headfitting.

Take the head measure and add 1'' (25 mm) to this (1'' is allowed for take up in the material caused by the seam allowance). Find the radii from the scale mentioned. Draw a line on the paper at least 8'' (20 cm) in from the edge of the paper. Place the drawing pin in the tape measure at the selected headfitting, not forgetting to allow for the hole in the tape, and place this pin and tape at the top of the line, and placing the pencil in the hole in the tape proceed to draw the first circle or headfitting. Add 2'' (5 cm) to this selected radius and draw another circle, this one constitutes the tip, and the facing. Mark in the centre front and centre back.

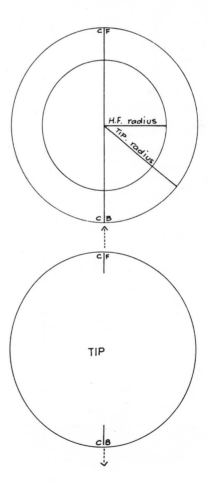

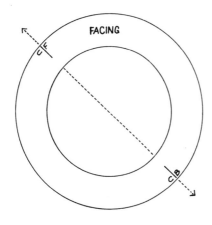

FACING

The facing may be made larger in one section and smaller in another, e.g. three and a half inches (9 cm) at the centre front and 1½'' (4 cm) at the centre back, and re-curving to meet the original circle.

The top may be broken into sections or circles. The facing may be broken into sections.

Mark the centre front and centre back on all pattern pieces.

When cutting out, place the centre front of one section on the straight grain of the fabric and the other section on the bias grain, e.g. the tip on the straight grain and the facing on the bias grain. The reason for this is to avoid the material stretching when the two sections are stitched together.

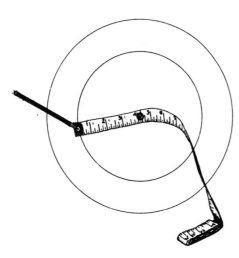

Place pattern paper under this construction and using a dressmaker's tracing wheel, trace around the two circles. Move the paper and trace the large circle only. Cut out these patterns, the disc is the tip or top of the beret and the other pattern is the facing or underneath.

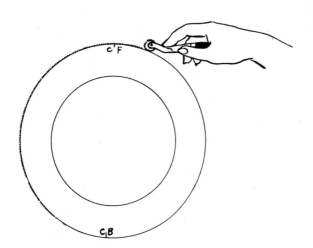

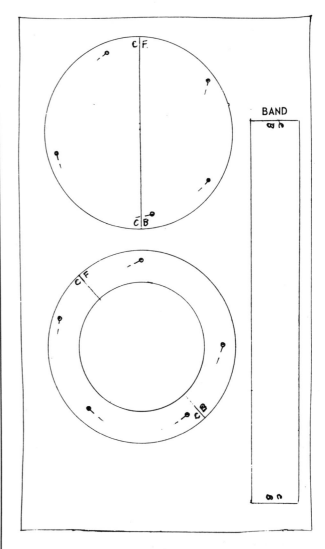

Interlining

Construction of Simple Beret

Cut a band to the straight grain the h.f. plus ½'' (13 mm) seam allowance by 2½'' (64 mm) wide. Cut out the sections of the beret with a ½'' (13 mm) seam allowance, in interlining and fabric. Mark around the outline of the pattern pieces on the interlining, then place the interlining onto the wrong side of the covering material. Tack the interlining and fabric together using the pencilled line as a guide.

Place right sides of fabric pieces together, and tack, and stitch by machine. End off the stitches by stitching back over two or three stitches or draw the thread to one side and tie off.

Remove the tacking stitches and cut away the surplus interlining to the machine stitching.

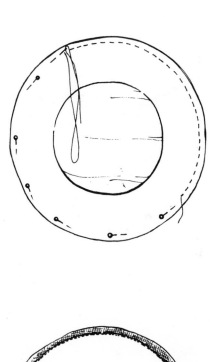

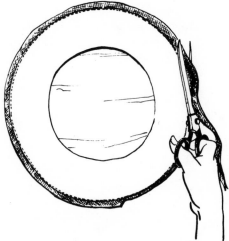

Make up a lining from the same pattern pieces, using a soft light fabric such as taffeta. This lining must be threadlined around the pattern pieces not pencilled.

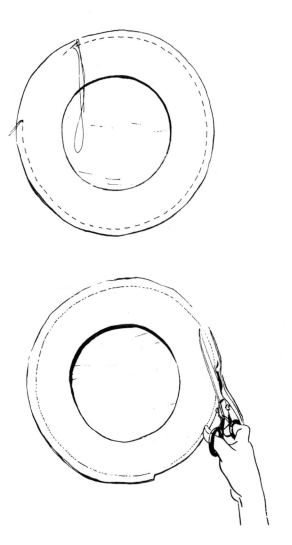

Place a pressing pad inside the beret, lightly press the seam open. Turn beret to right side and nick the headfitting every ½'' (12 mm).

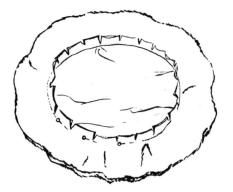

If dents are required along the seam edge, then ¼'' (6 mm) wide tape may be sewn inside along the seamline, the tape being smaller than the circumference of beret.

Insert the lining into the inside of the beret and tack around the headfitting.

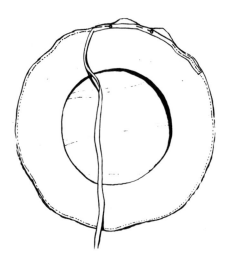

Stitch the seam in the band and press open. If the edge of the band is to show inside the crown, then this must be protected with overcasting stitches.

Place the band with the right side to the right side of the facing, pin and tack in position allowing ½'' (13 mm) seam allowance on the band. Machine stitch, ending stitching as previously described.

Start at the back, fit this ribbon around the headfitting of the beret placing berry pins at intervals vertically, making sure not to tighten the headfitting. Remove some of the pins and inverting the ribbon, back-stitch a seam. Cut away surplus ribbon leaving ½'' (13 mm) seam allowance. Press this open with the fingers and pin in position.

This ribbon head-band is stitched into position with an invisible stitch on the right side and longer stitch, approximately ½'' (13 mm), at the back. This stitch in this case is only taken through one thickness of the band.

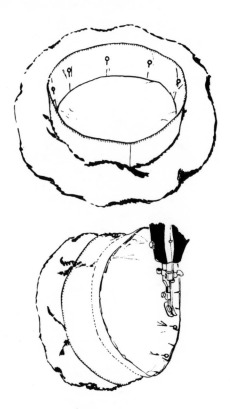

Cut away surplus fabric.

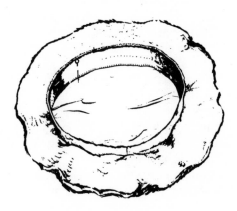

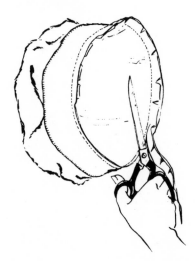

Turn the band over to the inside of the beret, tack into position. Machine stitch along the crease made by the seam, and tie off the stitches.

Select a length of grosgrain ribbon approximately 1'' (25 mm) wide and 24'' (61 cm) long. Wet this under the tap and mould it into a radius, using a hot iron.

Beret Variation

Many and varied designs may be constructed from the simple beret draft. The diagram shows how the facing may be alternated by extending the front and reducing the back. This facing may also have darts folded out to reduce the outer area and so make the facing stand up, for example, in the front and down at the back. In this case the area edge of the facing must be measured, take away 1'' (25 mm) and divide by 6. This formula is used to obtain 'tips' for all side bands.

The tip may be divided in sections or darted, in the latter case the radius for the tip would be larger to allow for the darts.

The band may be wide or narrow, shaped or plain. The beret may be mounted on willow and padded or draped, or it could have a brim.

The interlinings for the different types of berets are selected according to the finished effect desired, e.g. flannelette for the simple beret gives a soft draped effect.

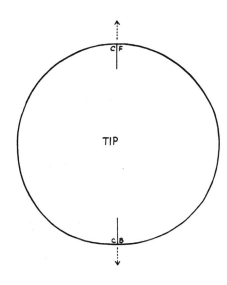

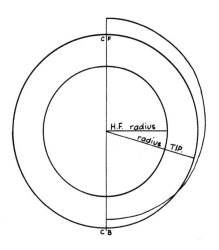

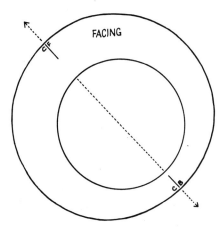

Pleated Beret

Construct the pattern from the simple beret draft. Shape the facing to the width desired. If the facing is required to stand up in front or droop at the back, then mark in darts in the appropriate sections. Fold out the darts by cutting down the centre of the dart and placing one line on top of the adjacent one. The outline may need recurving at this stage.

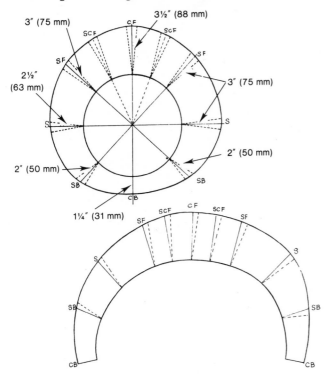

Measure around the area edge of the completed facing construction. Minus 1″ (25 mm) and divide by 6. The final sum is the radius of the tip.

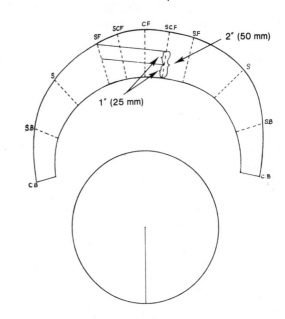

Mark the position for the pleat and cut and spread the paper pattern for the amount desired. When any cutting and spreading is required, then these cuts must lead to the edge of a pattern, otherwise the pattern will not lie flat.

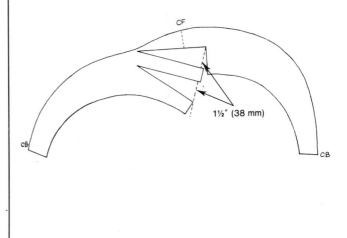

Cut out in interlining a facing without the pleats. This when stitched with the pleated fabric will form a support for the pleats. Cut a fabric facing from the pattern that was cut and spread. Also a tip in interlining and fabric. Pencil round the outline of the patterns on the interlining. Threadline around the fabric facing, marking the position of the pleats.

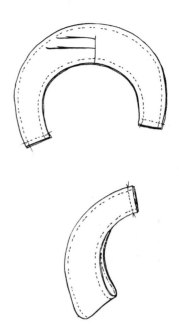

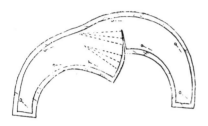

Pleat the fabric facing and stitch the small seam. Place the interlining to the back of the facing, pin and tack. Stitch the centre back seam. Press the seam open, cut away interlining to the machine stitching and trim the seam allowance.

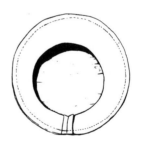

Sew the tip to the facing and trim the seam allowance. Small nicks may be made into the machine stitching if necessary. Make a lining from tip and plain facing, that is the one without the pleats. Finish with a plain band and moulded ribbon head band.

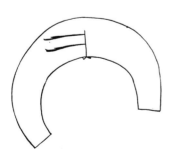

Draped Beret

This beret has extra fabric extending from the tip to form drapes over the facing. To construct this, find a quarter of the tip and extend the lines out sufficiently to allow the fabric to drape over the facing and to stitch into the band, allow for take up. For this example divide the quarter into three and rule lines from the quarter marks at the tip to the dividing lines of the extension. Cut this extended tip in fabric and the plain tip in interlining; and the facing in both fabrics.

Construct a facing and tip to the desired shape. The facing is darted according to design and the tip is constructed from the formula mentioned for the pleated beret.

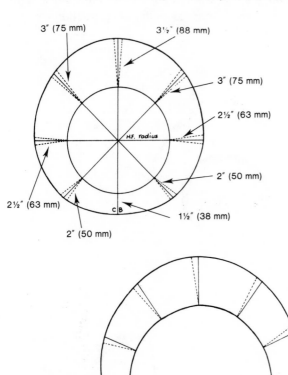

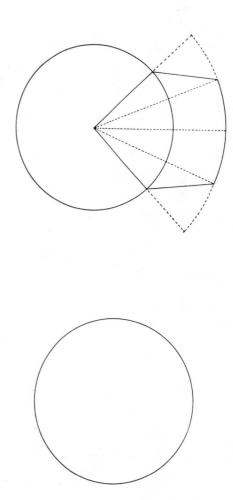

Outline the patterns as described previously. Stitch the centre back seam of the facing and press and trim it.

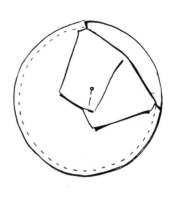

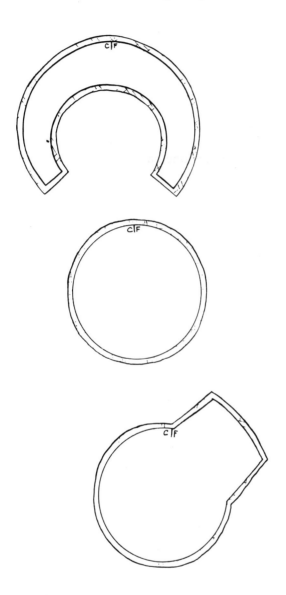

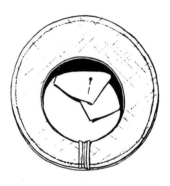

Stitch the facing to the tip, folding the extension out of the way. Trim the seam allowance as described for earlier berets.

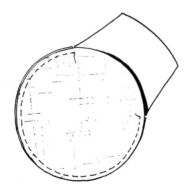

Pleat or gather the drape, pin and tack it to the headfitting. Finish with a band cut on the straight grain and a lining made from the pattern construction without the extension.

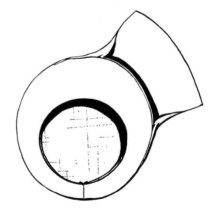

Basque Beret

This is a sectioned beret constructed from the simple beret draft. The facing sections are added to the tip sections and these are then cut as one.

Divide the simple beret construction into any number of sections by using the formula, twice the radius by twenty two over seven by one over the number of sections. In this case seven sections are required and the radius is 5¾'' (14.6 cm), therefore the formula is

$$\frac{23}{2} \times \frac{22}{7} \times \frac{1}{7}$$

The result obtained is the size of the sections.

This amount is marked off evenly around the outer circle. Trace off the tip and the facing, marking in the sections. Turn the facing section over to touch the marked section of the tip. The headfitting is now on the outer

edge. If the beret is shaped, then each section must be constructed and numbered, otherwise seven sections may be cut from the one pattern.

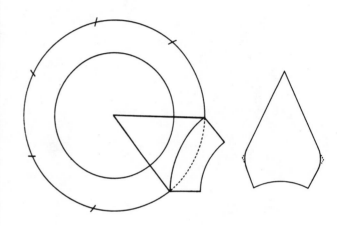

A variation of the sections may be made as indicated in the diagram. This is a swirled effect. Measure the curved lines to make sure they are equal in length.

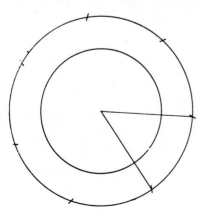

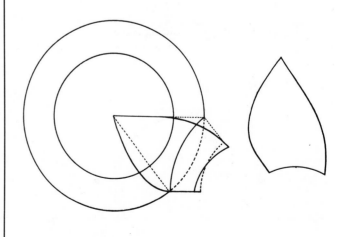

The sections are cut on the true bias, interlining and fabric. Pencil round the outline of the interlining defining the corners. Pin and tack the interlining to the fabric. Pin, tack and machine stitch two sections together.

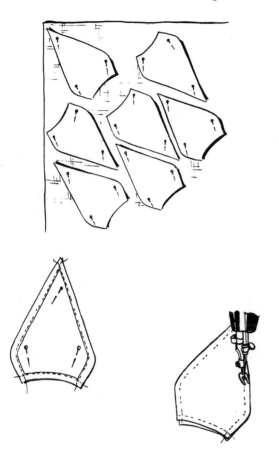

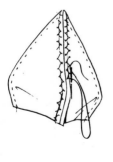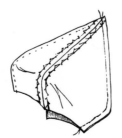

Cut the interlining to the machine stitching, trim the seam allowance, press open and catch stitch the seam allowance to the interlining. Place another section to this and repeat the above process. Make the other half of the beret in the same manner except that this will have four sections. Stitch these two halves together. Trim the seam as already mentioned.

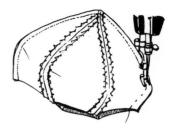

A band or brim is sewn to the headfitting and a lining made from the same pattern, as the covering.

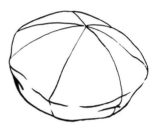

1. Satin hat trimmed with veiling and soft silk flowers *(see page 140)*

2. Shaded green chiffon hat mounted on stiff matching veiling *(see page 140)*

3. Milan straw model with satin crown mounted on a Leno shape. Satin edge and bows

4. Pink Thai silk on Leno or Sparterie *(see page 140)*

5. Two fur felt sailor hats made from capelines *(see page 140)*

6. Fine green wool hat trimmed with green satin cut on bias *(see page 140)*

7. Black hat with ostrich feather trim *(see page 140)*

8. Black and red fine wool with black satin trim, similar to Plate 7—this picture shows the back

Multiple Radii and Bias Strip Beret

This beret is an example of multiple radii and a bias strip. Many varieties of radii arrangements may be constructed in this way. This one was made with an interlining of handicraft felt, and stitched all over.

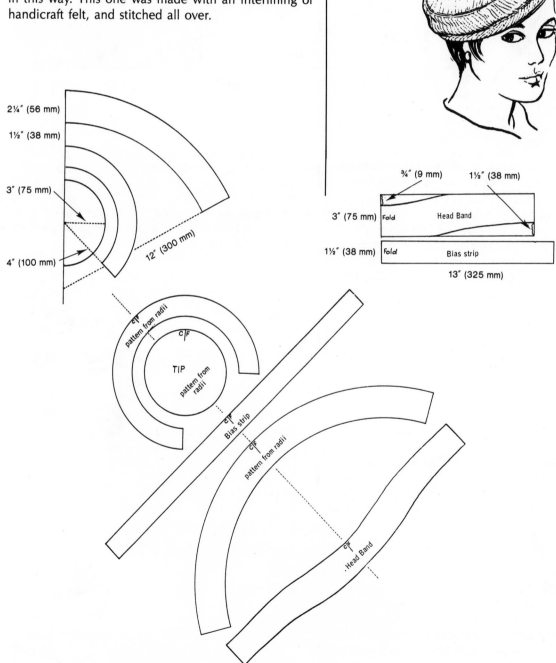

2¼″ (56 mm)

1½″ (38 mm)

3″ (75 mm)

4″ (100 mm)

12″ (300 mm)

¾″ (9 mm)　　1½″ (38 mm)

3″ (75 mm)　Fold　Head Band

1½″ (38 mm)　Fold　Bias strip

13″ (325 mm)

pattern from radii

C F

TIP

pattern from radii

C F

Bias strip

C F

pattern from radii

C F

Head Band

Bias Beret

Cut a bias strip of fabric, and interlining, the headfitting plus 1'' (25 mm) plus seam allowance by the depth desired plus seam allowance. Cut a tip the desired radius. Baste interlining and fabric together. Sew the edges of the bias strip and press open. Cut interlining to machine stitching. Divide this band and tip into four and mark with a thread of cotton. Gather the band to fit the tip matching the divisions. Cut away interlining to machine stitching. Note: Interlining to be used is according to the weight of fabric.

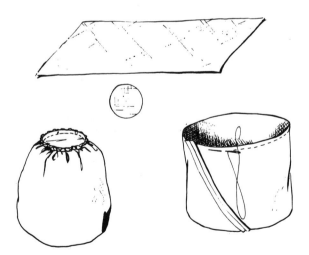

Make a lining to the same dimensions of outer covering. Cut a 3'' (7.5 cm) band of fabric on the straight-grain. Join the edges, press open, and with the right sides together, pin tack and machine sew the band to the crown. Turn the band to the inside and sew on the right side in the crevice.

Finish with a moulded ribbon headband.

Circle Beret

This consists of a circle of fabric, interlining and lining, to the radius desired. A band cut on the straight grain, join and place right sides together to the gathered circle. Finish as given for the previous beret.

Reversible Rain Hat

This hat is made with the brim all in one with the crown. Construct a pattern from a radius of 17″ (43 cm). The depth of the crown and brim is 8″ (20 cm), this allows 5″ (12.5 cm) for crown and 3″ (7.5 cm) for brim. But any depth or any radius may be used according to individual requirements. Reduce the curve of the arc at the centre back by ½″ (13 mm) to make the brim shorter in this area. Obtain a tip by using the formula mentioned earlier for all radii crowns.

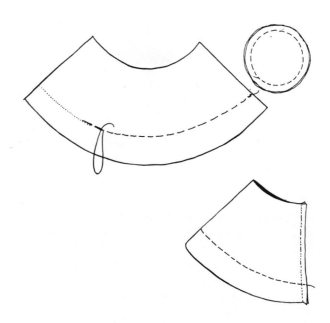

Press open the seam of the crown that is fabric only. Cut away the plastic to the machine stitching on the plastic covered one. Pin, tack and machine sew both tips to the crowns, leaving a section of the fabric open to turn through.

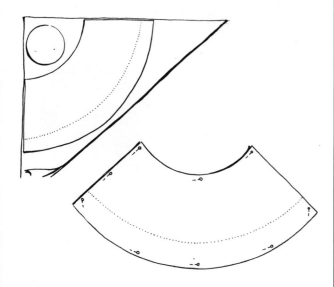

Cut two of each pattern in fabric and one in plastic, allowing ½″ (13 mm) for a seam. Threadline round the patterns and define the brim which is 3″ (7.5 cm) in the front and 2½″ (6.3 cm) at the back. Place the plastic to the right side of one tip and crown. With the right sides of the crown facing, stitch the centre backs of each.

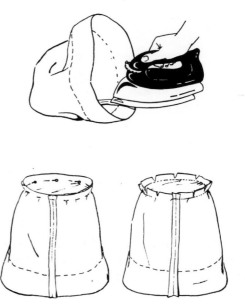

Trim and nick the seams. Place the two right sides of the brim together, pin, tack and machine sew. Turn one crown through the opening allowed in the other, and slip stitch the opening.

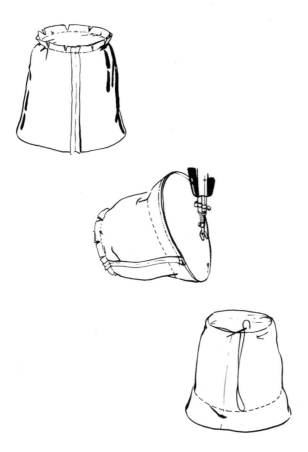

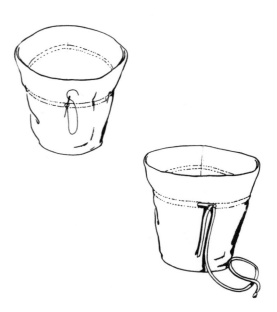

Place two metal eyelets either side of the crown. These can be inserted by using the same method as making eyelets in a belt and a special kit can be purchased.

Stitch two rows of machining round the headfitting. Make two eyelets in the fabric crown and thread a cord through and gather to fit the head.

Six Sectioned Crown

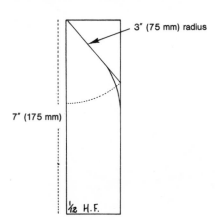

This crown may be made in any number of sections, and it may be deep or shallow. The sections may be stitched individually. The fabric may be in a range from tweed to satin. Interlining could be handicraft felt for the stitched job and canvas or vilene for a firmer effect.

The construction below is of half the pattern only. The head is measured over the top from ear to ear loosely, and this is usually 14″ (35.5 cm). Then firmly round the head and add 2″ (5 cm) for take up in fabric and to allow for a brim. If a band only is added then 1″ (25 mm) will suffice.

Draw a vertical line of half the depth required and square out at the base of this line for half of the section, in this case the hat is a six-section one, therefore the enlarged headfitting is divided by six. At the top of the line, draw an arc of a 3″ (7.5 cm) radius, because the head begins to curve at this point. Rightangle a line from the horizontal line at the base until it touches the arc. Draw a curve at this juncture to give a better shape.

Trace out the pattern and fold it on the vertical line. Cut out round the outline of the section. This gives a complete pattern. Cut six of these patterns.

3″ (75 mm) radius

7″ (175 mm)

¹⁄₁₂ H.F.

Construction

Place the patterns on the true bias of the interlining, that is providing the fabric has a weave. Vilene and handicraft felt may be cut any way. Pencil around the patterns, defining the corners. Cut out allowing ½″ (13 mm) for seams. Place the cut out interlining onto the wrong side of the true bias and cut out. Baste the two fabrics together by tacking around the pencilled outline. Define the corners.

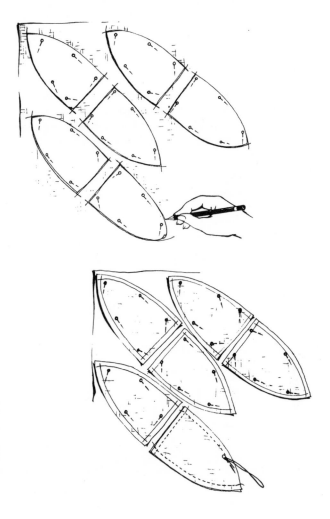

Pin, tack and sew two sections together. Cut away interlining to the machine stitching. Trim the seam and press open. Catch-stitch the seam allowance to the interlining. Place another section to these two and repeat the above procedure.

The brim is placed upside down on the crown or right sides facing, pinned, tacked and machine sewn. The interlining may be cut away to the machine stitching or merely trimmed to ½'' (13 mm) the same as the fabric. This will be according to the fit at this stage.

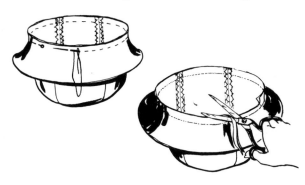

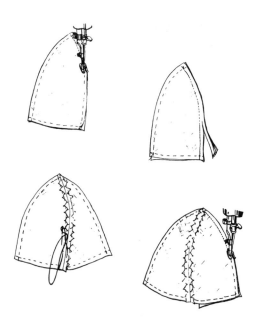

Trim the hat according to design.
Make a lining from the same patterns used for the outer covering. Pin and stitch this to headfitting. Mould and stitch a ribbon head band in position.

Stitch two threes together in this manner. Pin, tack and machine sew the two halves together. A pin placed horizontally at the top will avoid the points shifting. Care must be taken not to blunt or break the needle.

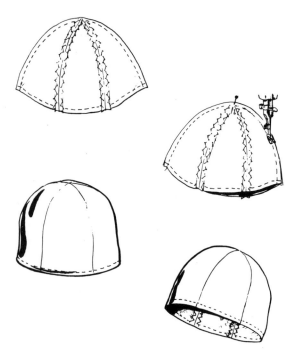

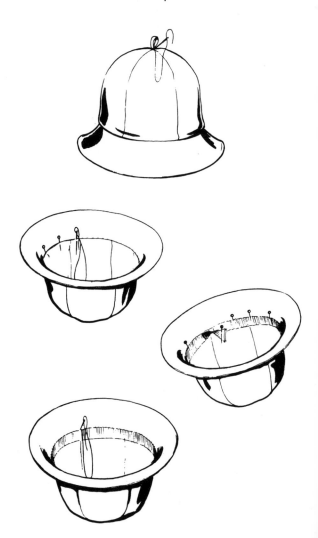

Three Sectioned Crown

Half of the patterns only are constructed; the horizontal line is the forehead to nape measure and the vertical line is half ear to ear measure.

Draw a rectangle of these measurements. Mark on the vertical lines at the top half of the centre panel. To obtain the side pieces, divide the panel line in half and mark to the right of this one quarter of the remaining headfitting, e.g. the enlarged headfitting is 24'' (60 cm), the centre panel is 4'' (10 cm) wide, twice this is eight, therefore 8'' (20 cm) taken from the headfitting leaves 16'' (40 cm). A quarter only of the headfitting will be constructed for the side pieces, for the obvious reason that the curve is to be uniform. In this case the measurement is 4'' (10 cm). Curve from this point to the panel line, keep the curve flat at the top. Measure this curved line and check to see that it is the same length as the panel line. Trace out the patterns and fold as indicated on the diagram. Cut out on the double paper around the outline of the side section and the panel. Cut out another pattern from the side section.

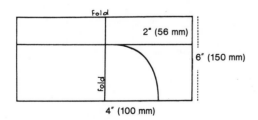

Place the patterns onto the interlining, the choice of interlining will be according to the type of hat. Canvas is suitable for a tweed or woollen fabric. Outline the patterns, and define the corners.

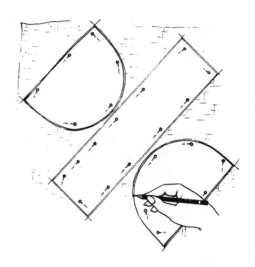

Cut out allowing ½'' (13 mm) for seams. Place the cut out interlining onto fabric, and cut out. Baste the two fabrics together by tacking round the pencilled outline.

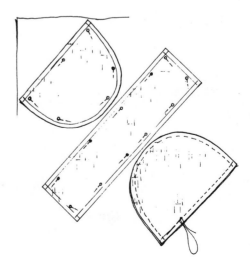

Pin the sections together and place the crown on a dome block to fit. Pin tack and machine sew the seam. Cut away the interlining to the machine stitching and trim and nick the seam.

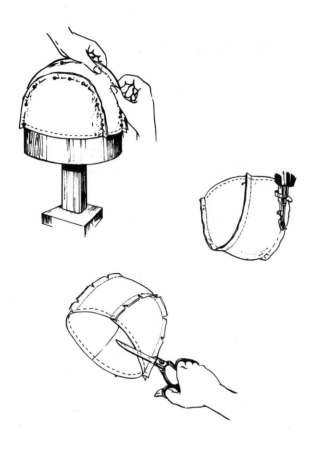

Machine stitch the crown to the brim with the right sides facing. Trim the hat at this stage. Fit the lining and sew it in.

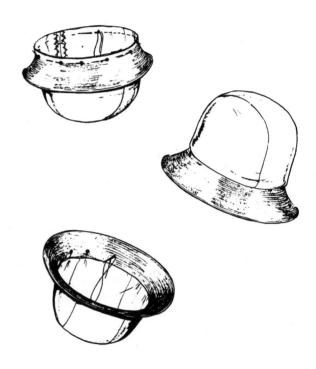

Carefully press the seams open, and catch the seam allowance to the interlining. Make a lining using the same patterns.

Finish the headfitting with a moulded ribbon head band.

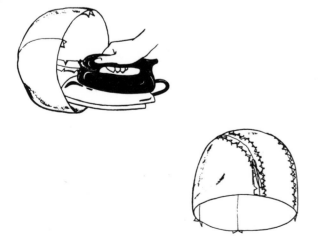

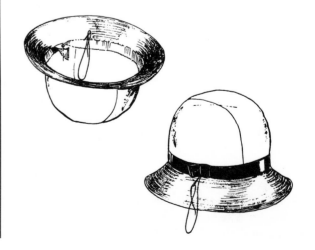

Unusual Sectioned Crown

This construction is suitable to use when an unusual sectioned crown is required. The same method can be used for a brim pattern using a brim block.

Cut a 14″ (35.5 cm) square of paper into the centre sixteen times. Place the paper over a wooden block and lap the paper to conform with the block.

Pencil the design required onto the paper. Carefully remove the paper and cut on the pencilled lines.

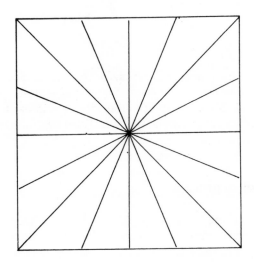

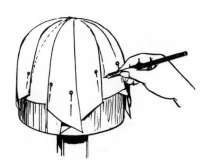

Completed pattern

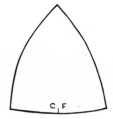

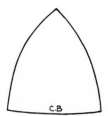

Baby's Bonnet

Materials required

⅓ yard (30 cm) cotton, silk, wool or nylon fabric. This is sufficient for the lining also (where suitable).

⅓ yard (30 cm) interlining, may be omitted.

Very fine thread suitable to fabric used, and a fine sewing needle.

⅓ yard (30 cm) double edged valenciennes edged beading.

⅓ yard (30 cm) 4″ (10 cm) ribbon.

1 yard (91 cm) valenciennes lace.

⅓ yard motifs, if required.

1 yard (91 cm) ½″ (13 mm) ribbon.

The above materials would be subject to fabric used.

The bonnet illustrated is a basic shape for the newborn infant. This one is for a special occasion and is made of breathing nylon with nylon tulle interlining, and nylon ribbon and lace to match. There are many and varied fabrics on the market which would make up very effectively, so long as the rule of harmony in the matching of lining, interlining and trimmings is obeyed. The stitching is hand done.

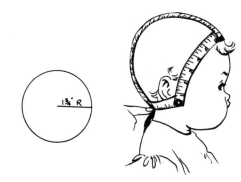

A larger bonnet may be made by obtaining suitable measurements. As the illustration shows, measure from forehead to nape and from the lobe of one ear to the lobe of the other around the face. From one lobe to the other lobe around the neck.

Pattern construction

Trace out the pattern and fold in halves, and cut out round the outline. The full pattern is obtained. Cut from the back to the face seven times, and spread these ¼″ (6 mm).

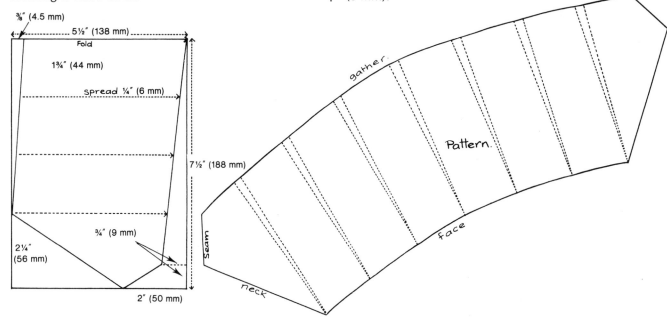

Place pattern on the centre front of the crown on the straight grain and the centre front of the tip on the bias. Cut two each of fabric and one of interlining. Threadline round patterns.

Divide the crown and tip into four. Baste the outer covering to the interlining, also the tip to a piece of paper the radius of the tip, this is to ensure a perfect circle when sewing. Satin stitch motifs or lace in position, or embroider.

Make a circle of lace to fit the tip. Gather the lace by drawing the thread on the selvedge. Lap one pattern over the other to join, and satin stitch around the outline, cut away surplus lace. Stitch the circle of lace, the selvedge to the threadline and back stitch.

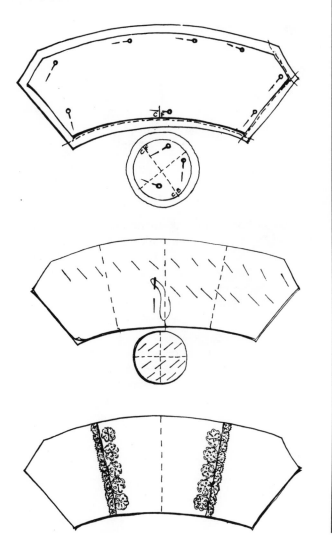

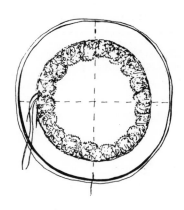

With the right sides facing, sew the seam of the crown. Cut interlining away to the machine stitching and press open. Place two rows of gathering at the back and draw this up to the tip. Match the four divisions on each. Pin, tack and back stitch.

Stitch ribboned insertion in position around the face, catching only the outer covering. Turn the edges of the insertion under the crown at the neck, encasing it between the folds of the lining and outer covering. Slip stitch the neck seam.

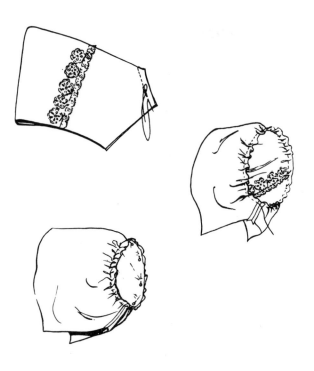

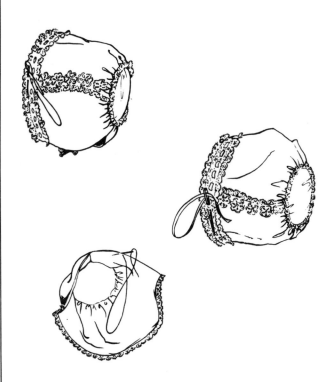

Make the lining in the same manner. Stitch around the face, with the right sides together. Trim the seam allowance. The lining needs to be ¼'' (6 mm) smaller to avoid showing around the face.

Gather a section of the ribbon, tie at both ends to form a rosette, or pleat the ribbon and form loops. Stitch these either side of the face at the neck.

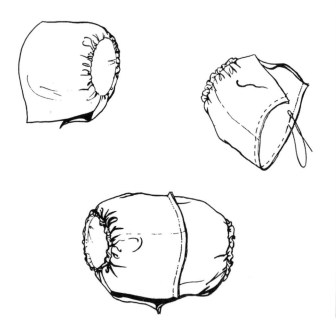

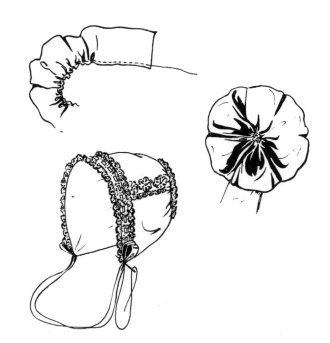

Winter Bonnet—1 Year

Construct a pattern from the dimensions indicated in the diagram. This bonnet has a horse shoe shape for the tip, and a turned back cuff may be cut in one with the crown and faced back or it may be separate, so that a contrast fabric may be used.

Cut in fabric one crown, one tip, and a facing, the shape of the cuff. Cut these in interlining and lining, with the exception of the cuff for the lining. The lining needs to be a ¼'' (6 mm) smaller than the outer covering so that it will not roll forward to show round the face.

Gather the crown between the marks indicated and match these with marks on the horse shoe.

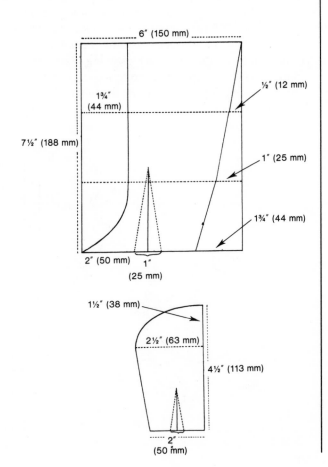

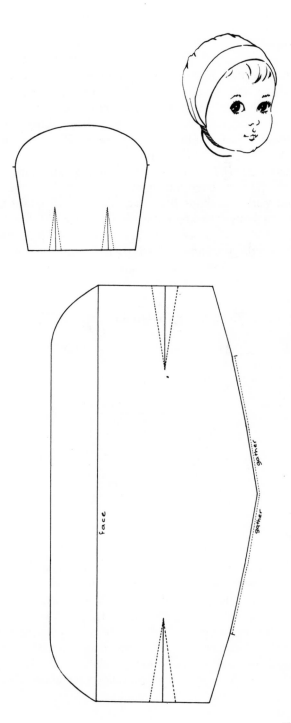

Toddler's Sunbonnet

Crown

Measure the child's head, from forehead to nape and around the face. Construct an oblong from the measurements, e.g. face 14'' (35.5 cm) forehead to nape 11'' (28 cm). Rightangle a line at half around face measure. Mark on the base line, either side of this line 2¾'' (7 cm) and 5'' (12.5 cm) up, square out 3'' (7.5 cm). Mark in these lines which constitute the flap. Mark out a ½'' (13 mm) extension on these lines and divide evenly and mark in scallops. Mark in on the centre front for ⅜'' (1 cm) to give shaping round the face. From the around face line mark on the vertical lines for 3¼'' (8.25 cm). Draw a diagonal line to the top of the flap. Trace out this pattern. It is the complete pattern for the crown.

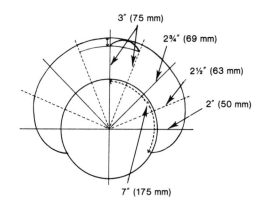

Cut the centre front on the straight grain, and the brim on the bias. The ties are cut 18'' (45.5 cm) long on the straight. Cut these out in stiffened cotton and once in plain fabric and once in patterned. Allow ½'' (13 mm) for seam. This is a reversible bonnet. Pencil around the outline of the pattern on the interlining. Baste the three fabrics together the outer covering with right sides facing and the interlining on top. Make the ties and turn them through to the right side.

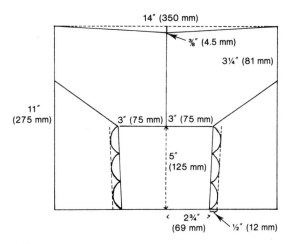

Brim

Draw a circle with a radius of 3½'' (9 cm). Rule a centre line. Rightangle a line from the centre of this line and bisect this angle. From the central line, measure round the circle for half the around face measure. Measure on the radiating lines the width of the brim, curving it to meet the face mark. Divide the area of the brim into equal sections. Mark inside the brim edge for ½'' (13 mm), construct a scallop. Make a template of this scallop and mark in the remaining scallops.

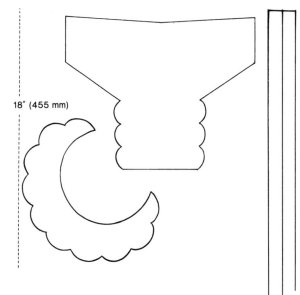

Threadline the around face.

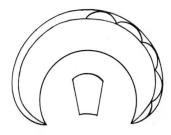

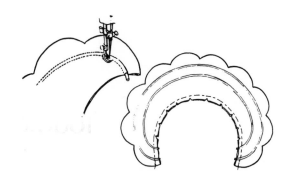

Tack the ties in position as shown in the diagram. Machine stitch right around the crown with the exception of the face; and around the brim edge. Cut the interlining to the machine stitching, and trim the seam allowance. Nick into the curves. Turn the crown and brim through to the right side. Press and tack round the edges.

Stitch a row of machine stitching ¾'' (19 mm) in from the indent of the scallops. Insert a length of bonnet cord close to this machining. Stitch the bonnet cord in position with the zipper foot attached to the machine. Insert another length of cord repeating the method as outlined above.

Nick the brim to the threadline on the around face.

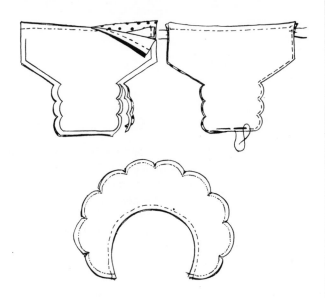

Place the patterned side of the brim to the patterned side of the crown. Pin, tack and machine stitch. Trim the seam allowance. Insert a length of bonnet cord on this seam and fold the seam allowance of the plain fabric over the cord. Tack to hold in position. Using the zipper foot, machine stitch.

Six buttonholes are made on the scallops; and the buttons are sewn on the straight side. The buttons to have a long shank to allow the bonnet to be buttoned on the reverse.

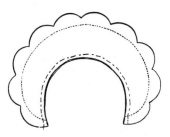

Drawn Bonnet—18 Months

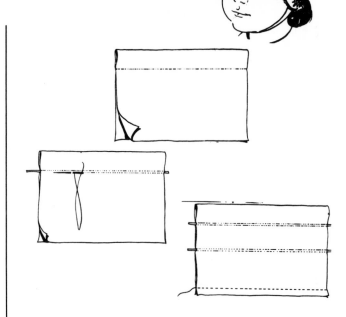

Fabric required 2 yards (1.83 m) organdie or lightweight fabric, approx. 3 yards (2.74 m) bonnet cord.

For the crown pattern, draw an oblong of half the around face by the depth of crown minus amount for the tip. Mark in on the back for 1¼'' (32 mm) and down for 1¼'' (32 mm). Draw this line in to form the back seam. Draw a line from this to the face line to represent the neck. For the tip, draw a circle of 1½'' (38 mm) radius.

Trace out these patterns, fold the crown in halves and cut around the outline to obtain the complete pattern.

The brim is constructed from a circle of 3'' (7.5 cm) radius, a larger radius may be used if more droop is required. Draw in the radiating lines to mark out the brim. Measure from the centre line around the circle for half the face. Trace and cut out the complete pattern.

Cut two crowns and tips. The crowns are cut on the bias and the centre front of the tip on the straight grain. Interline the crown with an appropriate fabric.

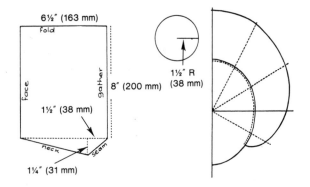

Cut a length of lightweight fabric, e.g. organdie, three times the area edge of the brim, by twice the width plus seam allowance. Fold the fabric in halves wrong sides facing. Stitch a row of machining along its full length. Place a length of bonnet cord between the folds of the fabric and against the row of machining. Attach the zipper foot to the sewing machine and stitch another row against the bonnet cord. Repeat this procedure at a suitable interval.

Draw the cords and gathering to match the outline of the pattern. Curving the raw ends into the face. Place another stitch around the face to outline the pattern.

Divide the tip and crown in four. Sew the back seam. Place two rows of gathering stitches in the back of the crown, and draw these to match the divisions on the tip, this facilitates evenness of gathers. Place the right side of the face of the crown to the brim face, pin, tack and stitch. Trim surplus seam allowance. Make a crown lining, place it inside the crown and slip stitch it around the face. This brim may also be used as a facing, omit the cord and insert gathering threads for drawing the fabric to the brim shape.

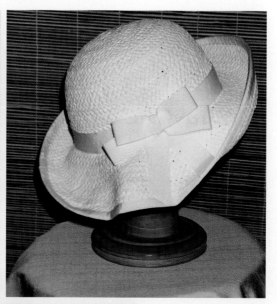

9. Six sectioned crown sports hat in red denim *(see page 148)*

10. White straw braid with petersham trim *(see page 148)*

11. Pink Breton pulled up sharply off the face (pages 71–72) and a tan straw hat shaped up a little all round *(see page 148)*

12. Paribuntal straw capeline trimmed with good quality satin *(see page 148)*

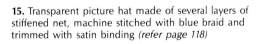

13. Cocktail or mother-of-the-bride hats *(see page 149)*

14. Black satin crown with see-through brim
(see page 149)

15. Transparent picture hat made of several layers of stiffened net, machine stitched with blue braid and trimmed with satin binding *(refer page 118)*

16. Cocktail hat in pewter coloured soft lamé trimmed with flowers and petals *(refer pages 133, 135)*

Hood—5 Years

Fabric required

1 yard (91 cm) for covering and lining
1 yard for interlining
1 yard lining
If contrast lining required—1 yard (91 cm)

Construct a pattern by drawing a rightangle on the left hand side of the paper. The vertical line is the half face measure 11½'' (29 cm), and the horizontal 14½'' (37 cm), for the top. Mark in on the base of the vertical line for 1½'' (37 mm) and square down for 1'' (25 mm) and for the neck square across for 8'' (20 cm). Draw an oblique line from this to the top to form the centre back seam. Place a 2'' (5 cm) wide dart on the neckline. Make this dart 2½'' (6.5 cm) high and 3½'' (9 cm) deep.

For the curve at the base of the hood, draw a radius from the top of the dart for 14'' (35.5 cm). Connect the arc to the front and back with oblique line. These lines are 9'' (23 cm) long. The point may be shaped at the back, therefore making it fitted. Curve for the front and back necks.

Cut outer fabric interlining and lining with the top on the fold. Sew the darts and split these open and iron flat. Baste the interlining to the outer covering and sew up the seams of both lining and covering. Cut seam allowance back to the machine stitching. Place right sides of bias and outer fabric together and stitch around the outer edge, leaving a section at the base of the cape open to turn through. Cut interlining back to make stitching and turn through to right side. Press the garment and slip stitch the opening.

N.B. Flannelette would be a suitable interlining.

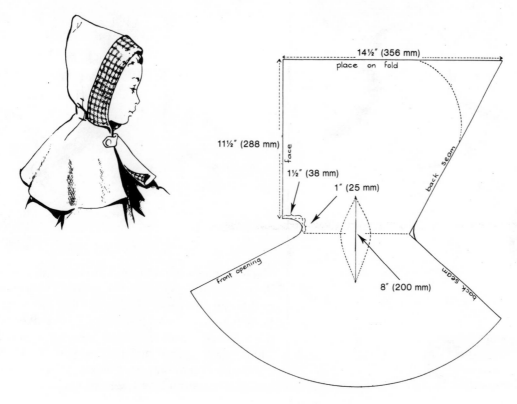

Straw Capeline

Finely woven straws such as Baku, Paribuntel and Sisol are usually made with a brim and are called a capeline. They are made from natural fibres, and require a maximum of moisture to block into shape. Imitations of these straws are made from synthetics, and these may be shaped with the use of steam. Currently (1990), the supply of fine straw has dwindled considerably. Readily available is Pari Sisol from China or the Philippines. Milan straw which is a fine braid comes in all colours. From Ecuador, good medium weight Panama straw with an excellent edge, hand woven by the women of that country, is available in 36 colours.

Select a capeline in one of the straws. Also a crown and brim block to the shape required.

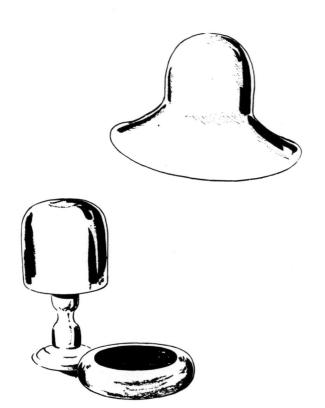

Dampen the straw with water or steam. If the straw is to be moulded into an intricate shape, then it may be immersed in warm water. Using the hands, mould the straw to conform with the crown block selected.

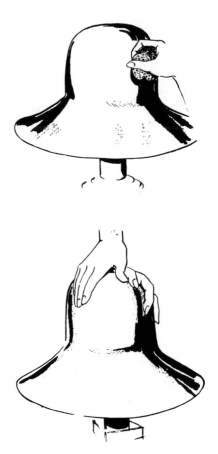

Place an elastic band around the headfitting and at the depth required and pin it in position. The use of berry or drawing pins will depend on the final trimming. Note: berry pins do not mark but drawing pins make holes and these would need to be cut away or covered by a trimming. It is sometimes necessary to use a wet cloth and warm iron to obtain a smooth surface. Straws burn easily, so care must be taken.

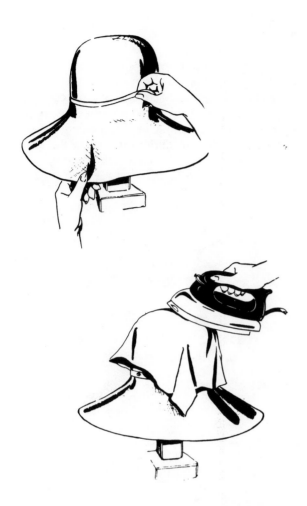

Select a brim block. Dampen the straw. Place the straw over the brim block (in this case a ring block). Pin the collar in position on the inside allowing ½" (13 mm), drawing pins are used. Mould the straw to the configuration of the block. Pin with drawing pins, if there is enough surplus to cut away, otherwise use berry pins to avoid marking.

Folds may be made in the straw, and this is done by using the fingers, moulding the folds into the desired shape. Carefully pin them in position with berry pins. Cut away the brim from the crown, allowing ½" (13 mm) for a collar on the brim. If the capeline is not deep enough, then willow may be inserted to allow for the extra height. An appropriate trimming would be needed to cover the willow. With a short neck, cut straw from side to side around back (as in the illustration), then lift brim. You may need to take ¼" (6 mm) off crown.

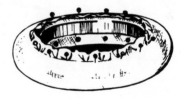

Mark centre fronts of brim and crown with a thread—or mark brim with tailor's chalk and cut away surplus straw. Stiffen inside of crown and brim with straw stiffener. If folds are made in the crown, then these are held in place with catch stitches, or several bar stitches.

Hemmed Edge

Another finish to a brim edge is to buttonhole stitch a wire ⅛″ (3 mm) in from the brim edge on the underside, making sure to have a good lap of wire at the centre back of at least 2″ (5 cm). Fold the edge of the straw over the wire and iron with a damp cloth placed under the iron. The straw must dry out under the heat of the iron for maximum results.

Buttonhole wire to crown and brim edges. The wire is placed just inside the edge. If the straw is firm it is more comfortable to use a bias piece of material around the brim. Dampen and iron the surplus straw that was cut away, and with the right sides together and the cut edges together, backstitch the straw strip to the brim edge. Make an open seam in the centre of the strip. Fold the strip over the brim edge, to form a binding, and backstitch in the crevice. Note: Have the finished edge of the straw strip on the edge that shows.

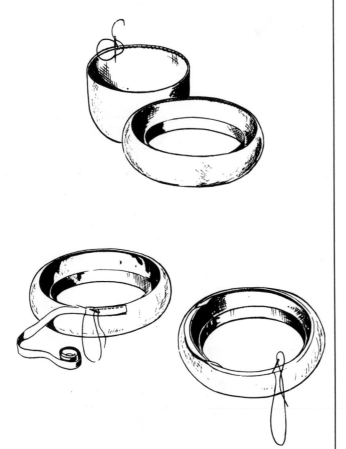

Fold the edge of the brim over once more and repeat the wet cloth and warm iron process.

Care must be taken not to spoil the shape of the brim.

Bound Edge
Fold a length of grosgrain ribbon in halves lengthwise, if necessary wet and mould it with a hot iron. Place the fold over the wired brim edge, stitch with a slanting stitch placing the needle diagonally in the crevice of the ribbon to keep the stitches invisible.

Place crown over collar of the brim and backstitch. These stitches will be covered with a trim. If concealed stitches are required, then the construction is similar to a fabric hat. Lightly stitch the trim in position.

To line the hat, thoroughly wet a 14'' (35.5 cm) square of cotton net. Place it on a wooden block with the straight grain on the centre front and centre back.

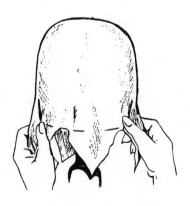

Place an elastic band around the depth of the crown to correspond with the straw crown. Allow to dry and then cut away surplus net. Pin the lining into position in the crown and stitch lightly. Fit and stitch a moulded ribbon headband in position at the headfitting.

The ribbon head band may be stitched to the brim before it is sewn to the crown.

A ribbon trimming should fit snugly, and if it is wide, it may need wetting and moulding (in the case of grosgrain), or draping if it cannot be wet. Stitch only where the two ends meet.

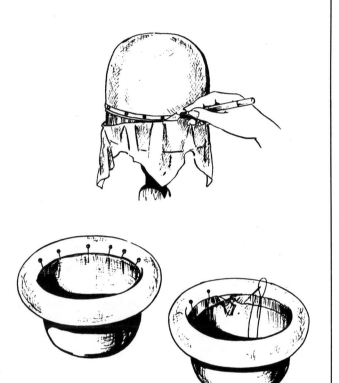

Straw Hood

The straw hood is suitable for a draped hat, a small brimmed model or a breton. A straw made of synthetic fibres does not require much moisture to shape. The very lightest steaming will suffice.

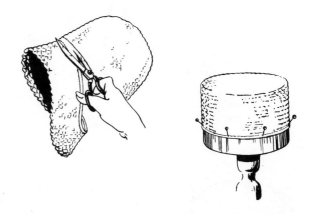

If a breton is required and the brim needs to be reversed, decide the depth of the crown and allowing ½″ (13 mm) for a collar on the brim, machine two rows of machine stitching around the collar. This prevents the straw from fraying when it is cut. Cut the brim from the crown and mould the crown on a selected block.

For a breton brim, select the appropriate block, and with the right side of the straw uppermost place it on the block pinning the collar to the inside curve of the block. For a droop brim a wooden collar is placed on the selected brim block. If a small hat is required with the brim all in one with the crown, then the crown is blocked first.

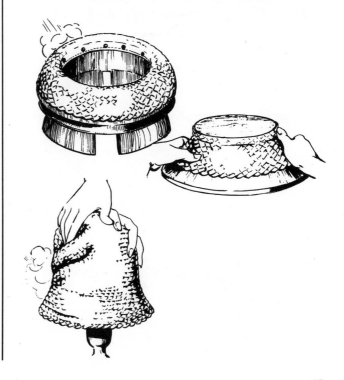

The crown with the block under it, can be placed onto a brim block and blocked all in one. If the blocks will not fit each other, allow the crown to dry and place the hood on the brim block without the support of the crown. Care must be taken in this case not to allow the crown to become wet with steam. Colour a length of millinery wire, with water colours to match the straw in the hood.

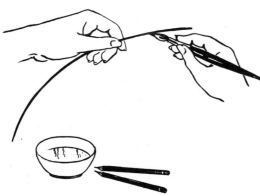

When the straw is thoroughly dry, stiffen the inside with straw stiffener. Stitch the crown to the brim with a backstitch. This will be covered with a trim. A moulded ribbon headband may be attached to the brim before it is sewn to the crown.

Buttonhole stitch a wire to the headfitting, and thread the coloured wire through the brim edge. Allow a good lap of wire at the centre back, otherwise the wire will poke through. Sew the wire together at the join in the brim.

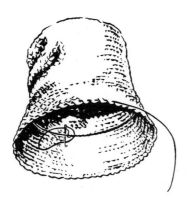

To line a straw hat, blocked net is used, this net must be cotton otherwise it will not mould. Cut a 14'' (35 cm) square, wet it and place it over a block to match the shape of the straw crown. Make sure the grain is running evenly. Place an elastic band in position at the depth of crown and allow to dry. Cut away surplus net.

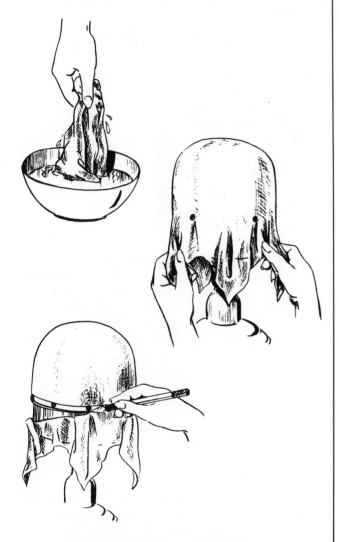

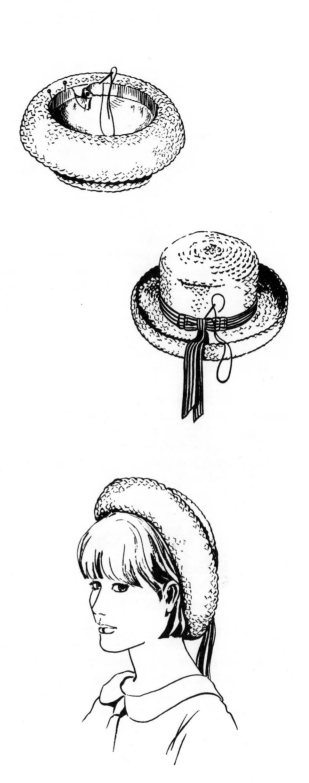

The hat is trimmed before the lining is inserted. The lining can be drying while the hat is being trimmed. A moulded ribbon head band is fitted, if not already done.

Straw Braid

This braid is purchased by the metre in many widths and colours; the edges are woven or sewn together to form a shape. The braid is stitched with raffia, Broder cotton or stranded cotton, in a colour to match the straw.

The amount of straw braid required for this hat would be gauged by the size of the hat and the width of the straw. Seven yards (6.4 m) of 1'' (25 mm) wide straw braid will be sufficient to make a small hat.

Select a wooden crown and brim, and starting at one end tie the end off. Place a draw thread for 6'' (15 cm) along the edge of the braid—this is then drawn to form a 'button'. Some braids have a draw thread, and this may be utilised. Many braids have a definite fancy edge which would be used as the outer edge.

Place the button wrong side down on the crown block; pin the braid in continuous circles for a section—the braid may be butted or lapped according to the type used. Stitch this section. The stitches are taken through a loop of the braid on top and the underneath is caught. If the braid is butted, then the edges are woven together.

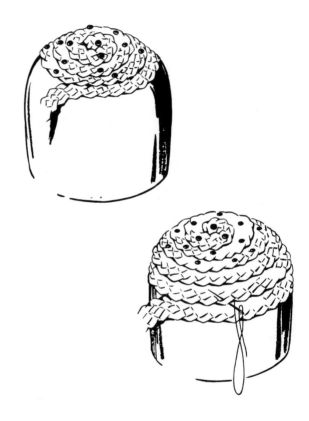

Continue pinning and stitching in this manner, until the desired depth of the crown is reached, then for the last lap, gradually decrease the width of the braid underneath the preceding row, until the end is lost, so making an even depth of crown all the way around.

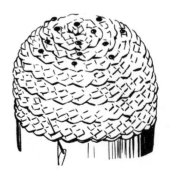

Brim

Place a collar on a brim block and start the braid on the collar, this forms a collar for the straw braid brim. Start at the centre back and take the braid around the collar until the back is reached. Gradually bring the braid down on the brim, tucking a portion of it under the previous row or butt it as the case may be. Pin, and stitch in sections the same as the crown. Lose the braid at the centre back. The brim may be shaped by decreasing the braid where required.

If the braid needs joining then it is woven by replaiting. Steam the brim lightly and crown lightly and allow to dry thoroughly.

Stiffen the inside with straw stiffener and allow to dry thoroughly. Take the spring out of a millinery wire, buttonhole this to the headfitting of the crown.

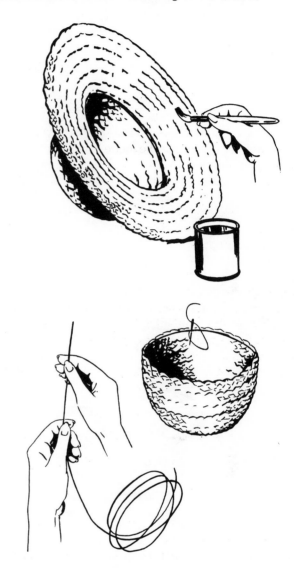

The crown can be stitched to the brim, weaving the stitches to make them almost invisible.

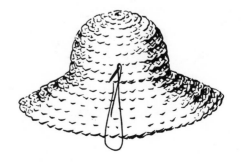

There are several methods of strengthening the brim edge:

1. Make a circle of wire, the area edge of the brim, lap the wire at the back for at least 2" (5 cm). Bind this wire with raffia or a strand of the straw braid. This is buttonholed to the wrong side of the brim.

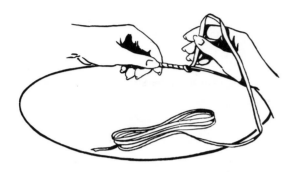

2. The wire is coloured with a water colour pencil and threaded through the brim edge.

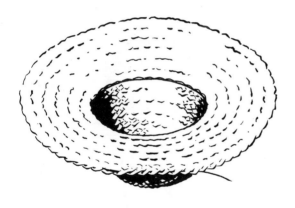

3. A wire is buttonholed just inside the brim edge, and this is covered with a length of the straw braid.

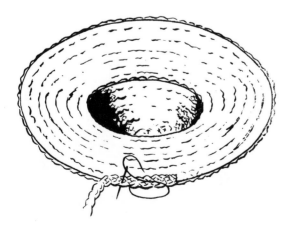

4. The wired brim edge may have a binding of straw braid to cover it.

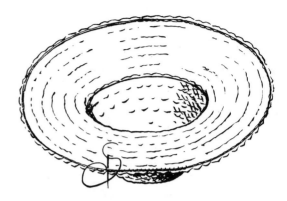

5. The edge of the straw may be folded over the wire and hemmed.

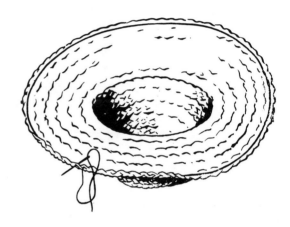

Velvet, satin, georgette or fruit or flowers are effective as a trim for this straw. Flowers made from the braid are also attractive.

After the trimming is applied the crown is lined with a blocked cotton net lining and finished with a moulded ribbon head band.

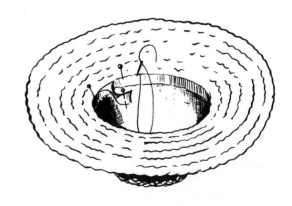

Curvette

Cut a square of willow 14″ × 14″ (35 × 35 cm) and dampen the straw side with a sponge. Place the willow on a selected crown shape, the headfitting plus ½″ (13 cm), wrong side to block. The straight grain of the willow is placed running from centre front to centre back. Insert four drawing pins, one each at the centre front, centre back and sides. The reason for positioning the pins at these points is that the willow will not stretch on the straight grain. Place an elastic band at the required depth of crown.

Pull at the bias points, to remove the folds. Steaming may be required at this stage to soften the willow. Allow the shape to dry thoroughly, and it is better for willow to dry out naturally, as it becomes brittle under artificial heat.

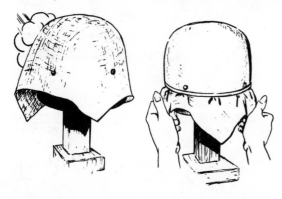

To mark the depth of the crown, measure from the base of the block and mark with a pencil. The shape is removed carefully from the block and the headline is cut

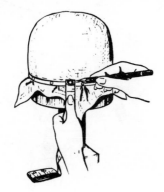

with the scissors around the shape. Iron a length of bias binding, and fold this over the wired shape, stab stitch.

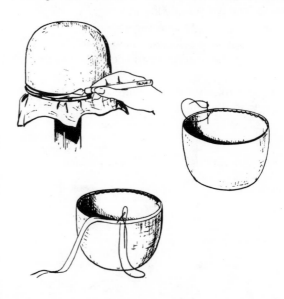

This method is suitable for shallow crowns and many different shapes may be made.

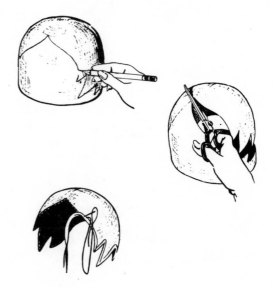

Moulded Willow Brim

1. Mark 6″ (15 cm) wide strip on bias of willow.
2. Cut the willow strip the full length of the fold.
3. Immerse the willow quickly in water.
4. Fold the willow right side together.
5. Iron to shape of a selected russel board brim.
6. Pencil round the headfitting and centre backs on both sides.
7. Cut away surplus willow at centre backs. One centre back is cut on the pencil line.

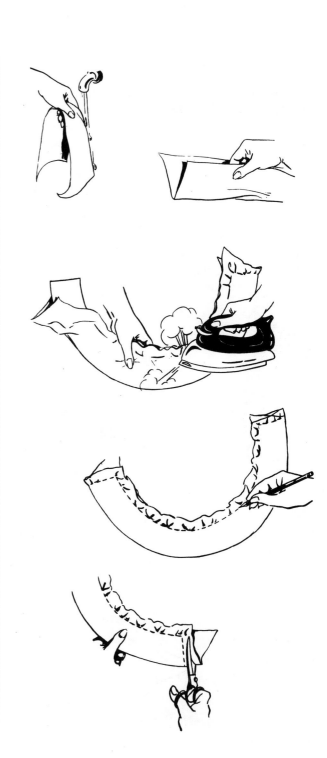

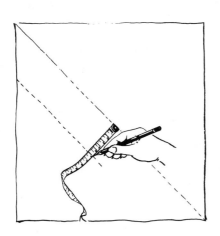

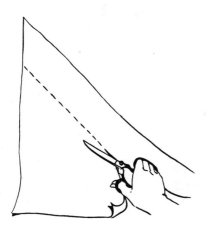

8. Lap the willow at the centre backs, matching the pencilled marks. Stab stitch on both sides.

9. Join a wire to the circumference of the brim edge.

10. Place wire in fold of brim edge and buttonhole on outer edge to hold the wire in position.

11. Stab stitch a tape at the headfitting, allowing 1'' (25 mm) extra for take up in fabric.

12. Fit a bias strip of fabric, face down to the brim edge, pin and tack and fit again.

13. Machine sew the join. Cut to half inch seam allowance and press open. If the fabric is velvet, then steam the seam open.

14. Place the covering fabric onto willow brim and pin at headfitting. Stab stitch covering at headfitting.

15. Cut away surplus fabric at the headfitting, leaving ½'' (13 mm) collar. Nick into the headfitting.

16. Some fabrics require an interlining, and this brim may be covered first with a light fabric, wadding, vilene or foam plastic. These to be cut to the shape of the russel board brim and stab stitched to the frame.

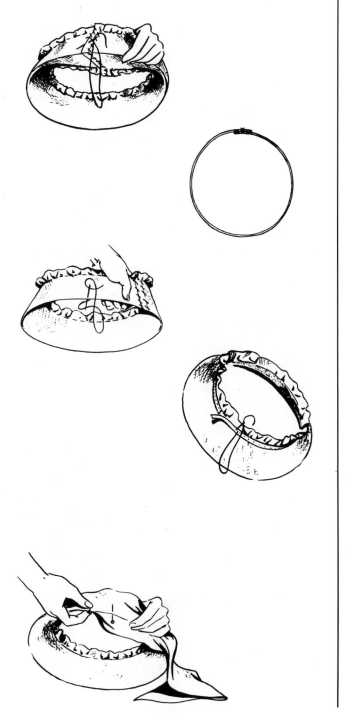

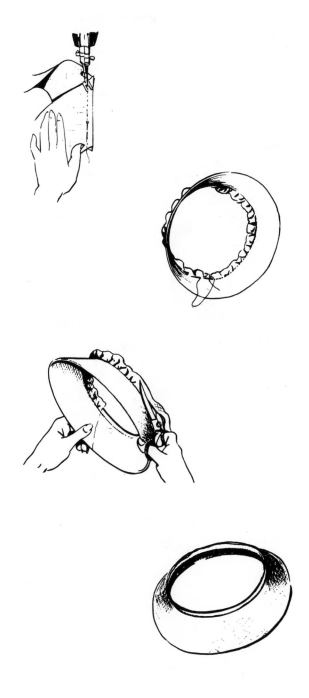

Willow Crown in Two Sections

This method is suitable for a deep crown.

Using the method described for curvette, block a small tip. For the side band, cut a strip of willow on the true bias, the full length of the willow by a little wider than the depth required. The reason for the extra width is that all materials reduce their width when stretched on the bias. Dampen this bias strip and mould it around the block, allow ½'' (13 mm) for a seam. Pin in position and allow to dry. Lap the willow for ½'' (13 mm) and diagonally stab stitch each edge to form a seam.

Wire and bias bind the edge of the tip, and wire and bind the base of the crown, and the top edge of the crown. Cover the tip with fabric and diagonally baste this to the binding. Fit the crown with bias fabric.

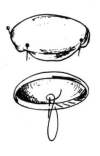

Machine sew a join in the bias side band. Trim the seam and press open. Diagonally baste the covering fabric to the bias binding on the wrong side. Place the tip in position and slip stitch.

N.B. Bias binding is ironed flat for use.

17. Blue Panama Breton trimmed with box pleats caught in the centre *(refer page 127)*

18. Orange Panama Breton turned up a little all round with wide floral polyester material trim *(see page 149)*

19. Light brown off-the-face Panama, petersham ribbon around brim *(see page 149)*

20 and 21. Panama hats showing different blocking methods and trims

22. Fun evening confection—a blue round pillbox covered in self petals, underlined with pink silk; spikes of matching beads

23. Hat brim on crown covered with multi-coloured silk triangles *(refer page 122)*

24. Sequin whimsy trimmed with tiger lily and veiling *(see page 149)*

25. Pillbox variation trimmed with petersham and veiling *(see page 149)*

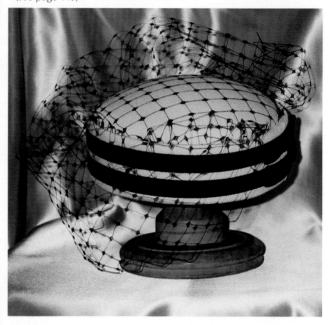

Willow Breton

Dampen a large square of willow on the straw side; place this side down on a breton block. Have the straight grain running from centre back to centre front. Smooth any wrinkles by pulling the bias. Place an elastic band round the brim edge. Cut out the centre and allow ½'' (13 mm) for a collar.

Pin this collar onto the headfitting. Allow the willow to dry naturally, and then cut away the surplus from the brim edge. Buttonhole a wire around the edge, stab stitch bias binding, which has been ironed out, to the wired edge.

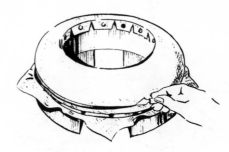

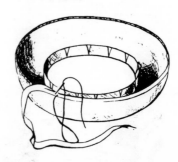

Make a ½'' (13 mm) wide collar from a bias strip of willow, and buttonhole a wire around the base.

Place this on the outside of the brim collar and stitch with cross stitches.

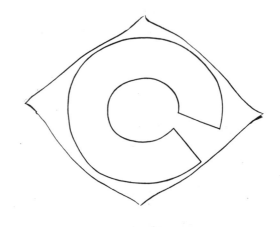

To obtain a pattern for the brim, mould aluminium foil inside the curved shape.

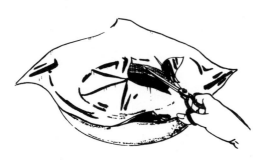

Alternatively the outer brim may be covered without a seam using the method as illustrated, stretching the fabric over the brim and cutting the centre out. This is suitable for fabrics with the maximum of stretch.

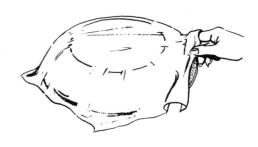

Open the foil at the centre back to allow it to lie flat on the paper. Pencil around the outline. Place this pattern with the centre front on the bias of the fabric. Cut out and allow ½'' (13 mm) for seams. Machine sew the centre back seam; this is the covering for the outer brim. This is diagonally basted to the bias binding on the inside of the brim edge. This method is used where the fabric has not much stretch.

The pattern obtained from the aluminium foil is used for the inner brim also. Machine sew the seam. To hold the fabric in the curve it may be necessary to use glue. Apply the adhesive and wait until it is 'tacky', make sure it is spread evenly using tissue paper to spread it. Smooth the fabric with the fingers to eliminate wrinkles. The edge of this is either turned and slip stitched or if the outer covering is not yet applied then turn it over the edge and diagonally baste to the bias binding.

Line with an appropriate lining. Finish with a moulded ribbon head band.

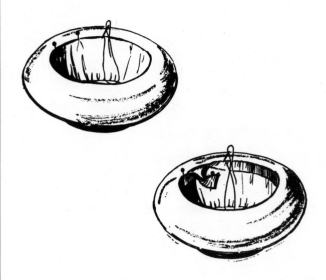

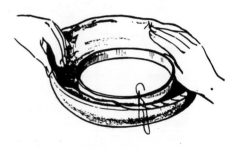

The edge may be finished with a piping. In that case the piping is applied before the outside covering, and the covering is applied with a bedding stitch. To make the piping cut narrow strips of fabric on the true bias, fold the fabric over bonnet cord, the right side uppermost, and stitch using the zipper foot on the machine. This is placed at the brim edge and diagonally basted, crossing it at the back. Place the crown over the brim and back stitch. Trim at this stage.

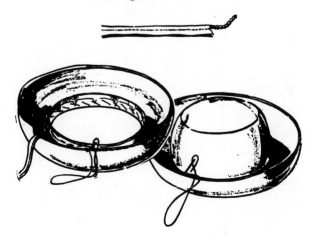

Willow Brims

Measure round the curve of the block, from the inside, which is the headfitting to the brim edge, also the area edge. Cut a strip of willow on the true bias, a little more than the width required: the reason for this is because all material when cut on the bias and stretched will take up in width. It is usual to cut the full length of the willow when it is cut on the bias. Dampen the willow on the straw side, place this side against the block, and pin the headfitting first. Take the willow right over the curve and pin inside. Allow the willow to dry naturally. Measure the depth of the brim required, pencil this and then cut away the surplus willow. The brim edge is wired with buttonhole stitch and bias binding is ironed flat and stab stitched to the brim edge covering the wire.

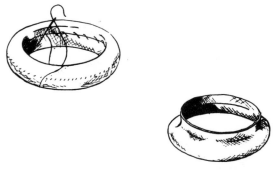

The illustrations show the various types of brims that may be made from the ring block and a bias of willow.

For a rolled brim, a wire is buttonholed along the centre on the inside. The two raw edges are stitched together, or the roll flattened and the raw edges will form a collar.

A ½" (13 mm) wide bias strip of willow is made into a collar and wired at the base; this is used to strengthen the collar of willow brims.

Willow Pillbox

Select a collar to the headfitting plus ½'' (13 mm). Place the collar on the wrong side of the willow with the centre front on the straight grain. Pencil round the outline of the block. Cut this out allowing ½'' (13 mm) for seam. Buttonhole a wire to the pencilled outline on the willow. Nick into the wire at ½'' intervals.

Place the tip inside the crown and stitch with cross stitches.

Buttonhole a wire to the headfitting and bind with bias binding which has been ironed flat. The binding is applied with a stab stitch. Bind the tip with bias binding. Diagonally baste tip covering to bias binding.

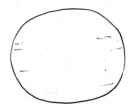

Cut a bias strip of willow the headfitting measure plus ½'' (13 mm) plus seam allowance by the depth required. Join the seam with a diagonal stab stitch, a row on each edge.

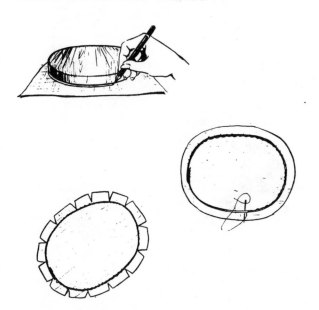

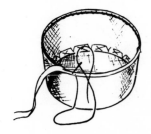

Fit a length of bias fabric to the crown, allow for seams on all edges. Join the seam, trim and press open. Place fabric onto shape and tuck seam allowance in at the top, this should fit firmly and is not stitched.

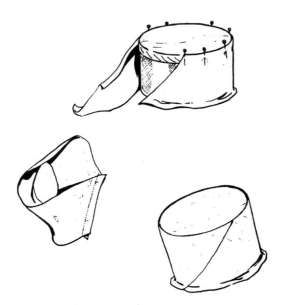

Turn the seam allowance on the lower edge to the inside and diagonally baste to the headfitting. Make a lining to the dimensions of the willow shape. Fit and slip stitch the lining in position.

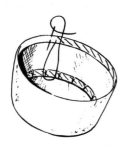

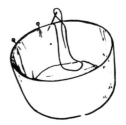

Stitch a moulded ribbon head band in position. If a trimming is required then this is applied with tie stitches before the lining.

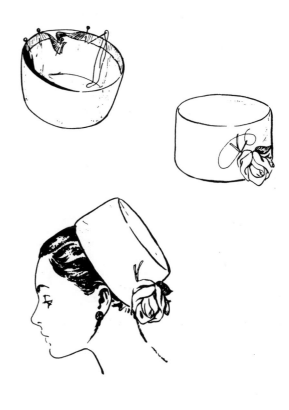

Willow Whimsy

Cut a 3″ (7.5 cm) wide strip of willow on the true bias. Damp it on the straw side and fold this in. Mould the willow round the block to a design.

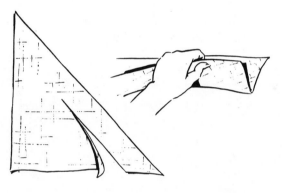

Diagonally baste the fabric to the binding; bring the other edge over, turn under and slip stitch. An elastic fitted at either side will give security. Elastic with small hooks can be purchased to hook into the cloth or the elastic may be twisted and knotted and sewn in position. The head fitting is finished with a moulded ribbon head band.

When the willow is dry, trim it to give a good outline and buttonhole a wire right round the edge, starting at the centre back. Pad with foam plastic or wadding. Cut and fit a bias strip of fabric to completely cover the shape.

Draped Toque on Canvas Foundation

Measure down the selvedge, for approximately 18''
(46 cm), of linen canvas and fabric. The weight of the
fabric will determine the length. Baste these two together.

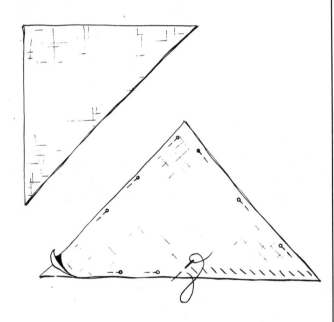

Fold the triangle in halves and from the fold, measure
the headfitting plus 2'' (5 cm) or more if a rolled effect
is desired. Stitch from this point to the edge, and along
the selvedge, rounding off slightly. The point may be left
on if desired. Cut away surplus fabric. Cut canvas to
machine stitching.

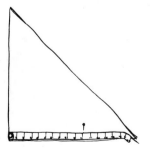

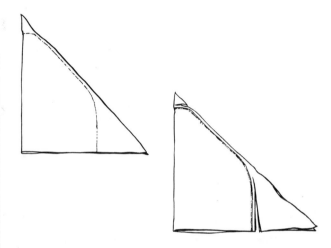

Drape on a dome block. Baste folds in position
temporarily.

Lightly catch the folds in place on the inside. Fold a narrow bias strip of willow. Dampen it and mould it round a dome block.

Place this shape round the crown and diagonally baste them together. Trim the hat. Line with a sixteen pleat lining and a moulded ribbon head band.

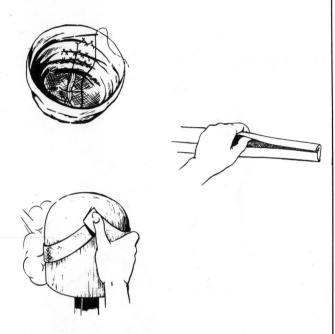

Buttonhole a wire in the folds, and stitch the edges together. To give a soft effect pad the shape with foam plastic, wadding. Cut a bias strip of fabric, twice the width required, plus seam allowance, plus take up. Stitch this to the shape having the join just inside the headfitting edge; so that it will be covered with the head band.

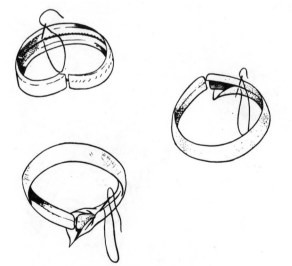

Draped Toque with Faced Corner

Make a willow shape, this one is shaped up at the front. Cut a triangle of fabric, allowing enough depth for draping into pleats, some fabrics take up more than others. Cut a section off one corner and placing right sides together stitch around the outside edges.

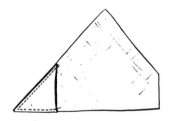

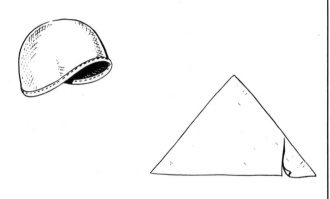

Fold the triangle in halves and stitch the top corner. Turn the drape through to the right side and place it onto the shape. Pleat the edge of the raw corner and pin this to the centre of the shape.

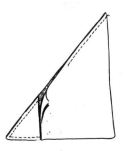

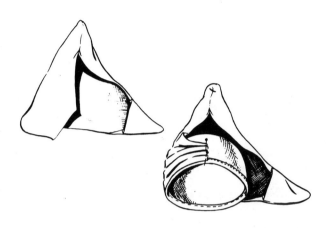

Draw the faced corners through a rouleau or buckle. The corners can be positioned in various ways. Line with a sixteen pleat lining and moulded ribbon headband.

Draped Toque—One Bias Strip

Make a shape of willow and pad it with foam plastic or wadding. Cut a bias strip of fabric to fit the base. Stitch the ends together and press open. Place the fabric over the edge of the shape and diagonally stab stitch it in position. Make up a triangle of fabric and drape this over the top. Stitch the folds, care must be taken not to allow the stitches to show.

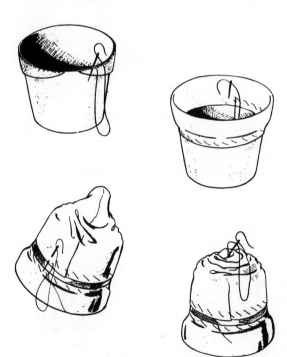

Cut bias strips of fabric and pleat in the right hand, pin and tack the folds. With a firm hand stretch the fabric to encircle the crown.

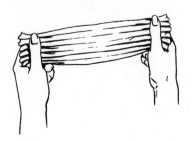

Continue placing bias folds around in this manner, hiding each preceding end with the following fold. Tuck the final end under the preceding fold. Line and finish the head-fitting with a moulded ribbon headband. Contrast of texture, and contrast or gradation of colour could be used.

Draped Toque—Two Piece

Make a shape from willow, cap net, or canvas. The foundation will vary according to the weight of fabric used. Cut a bias strip of fabric, long enough to encircle the base and wide enough to give the desired drapes. Cut an oval large enough to fit the tip of the crown allowing for gathers in the width.

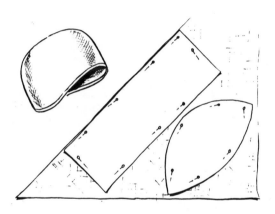

Gather the oval at the points. Stitch these to back and front. Stitch bias strip to the base of the shape. Pleat the bias strip and stitch in between the folds. A drape must look as though it has not been stitched.

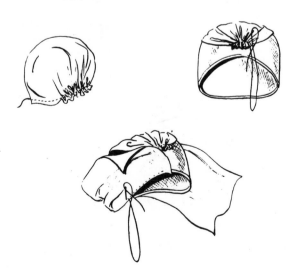

Finish the edge with a narrow bind of bias fabric, stitch with right sides together and then turn the bind to the inside. Diagonally baste it to the bias binding. Finish the pleats with a folded tab and bow ends. Line with a sixteen pleat lining and moulded ribbon headband.

Rolled Brim in Canvas

A firm elasticised canvas is used for this brim. Cut a bias strip of canvas 6'' (15 cm) wide by the headfitting plus 6'' (15 cm). Sew the centre seam and press open. Fold the strip lengthwise and place a wire between the folds. Make sure there is a good overlap of wire. Buttonhole the outside edge, this is done by inserting the left hand in the folds to hold the wire in position.

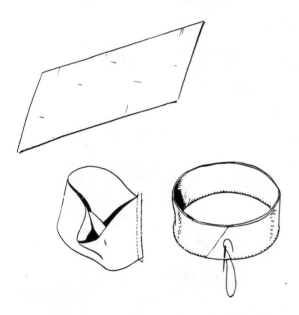

With a double thread of thick cotton gather the raw edges to the headfitting plus ½'' (13 mm). Pin the brim to a wooden block, steam and mould to the shape required. The gathers may be concentrated in the one area to give less turn up in that spot.

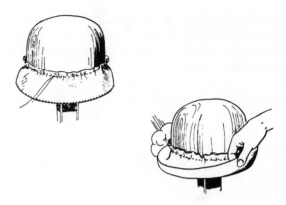

Stiffen the canvas, with straw stiffener whilst it is still on the block. Pad with cottonwool to hold the shape. Allow to dry thoroughly. Cover this brim with a 6'' (15 cm) wide bias strip of fabric in the same manner as described for the previous canvas brim.

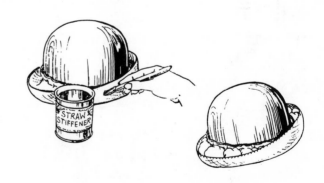

Cap Net, Leno or Marli

Cap net may be purchased by the yard in various colours and patterns. It is thoroughly wet and blocked to a desired shape. It is used as a foundation for petals, leaves, organza or similar lightweight fabrics.

Select crown and brim blocks of desired shape, and place a thin plastic or cellophane over to prevent the cap net from sticking to the block. Care must be taken if using plastic because if the cap net is stiffened with the plastic underneath the straw stiffener it will disintegrate the plastic. The cellophane tends to adhere to the cap net. Wet a square of cap net large enough to cover the block. Place it on the block with the straight grain centre front to centre back. Place an elastic band round the depth of headfitting and smooth out the wrinkles.

Pin the elastic in position and allow the shape to dry thoroughly. Cut away the surplus cap net. Stiffen the shape with straw stiffener.

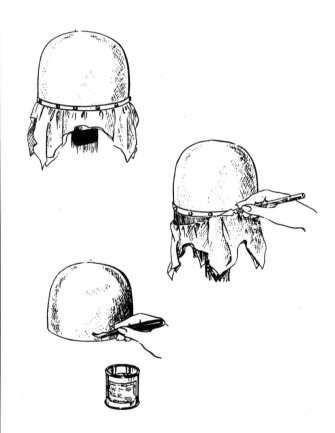

Block the brim in the same method as outlined above.

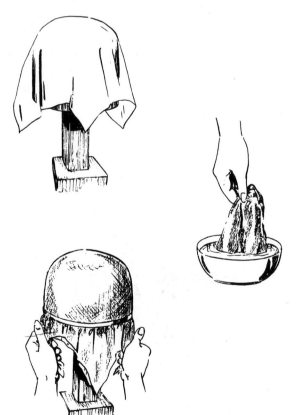

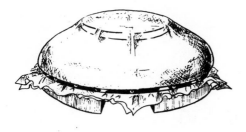

When the brim is dry, trim away the surplus cap net.

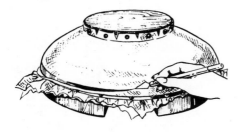

Stiffen the brim with straw stiffener. Buttonhole a wire to the crown and brim edges and fold bias binding over the wire stab stitching it in position.

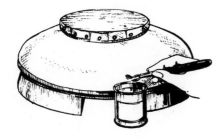

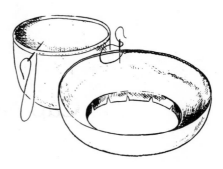

Place the crown over the brim and back stitch with a stab stitch.

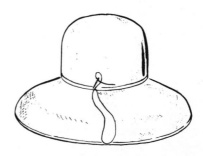

The hat may be covered according to taste. The lining is blocked cotton net and finished with a moulded ribbon head band. **Note:** If petals or leaves are stitched to the hat all over, then care must be taken not to have long threads of cotton criss-crossing. The threads must be finished off and started again.

Guipure Lace

Place thin plastic over selected crown and brim blocks. Mix instant starch to a thick consistency and wet the lace with this. Place the lace over the crown block, with a straight grain to centre front and back. Place an elastic band at depth of crown. Smooth out any wrinkles.

When the lace is thoroughly dry, cut away the surplus lace. Where the patterns of the lace overlap, where it was pulled on the bias, carefully cut around the pattern and overlap lace and satin stitch round the pattern.

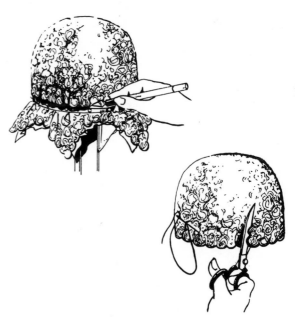

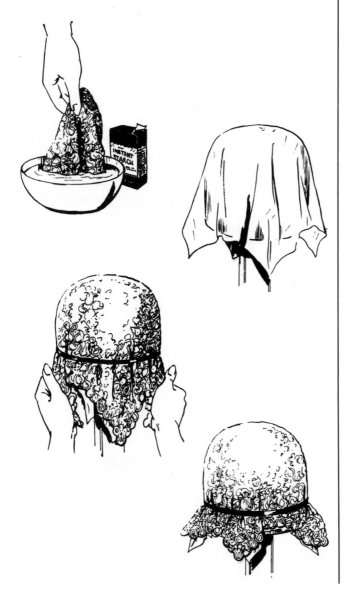

The brim is constructed in the same way as the crown, but cuts are made into the headfitting.

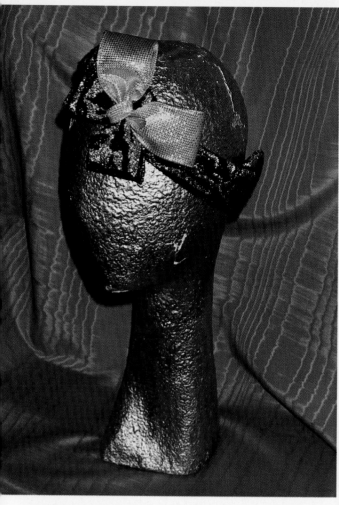

26. Willow whimsy in black and gold, using contrasting material; veiling could be added *(refer page 93)*

27. Pink Thai silk hats trimmed with hand-tooled stiffened roses *(see page 149)*

28. Silver/white wired whimsy *(see page 149)*

29. Cocktail hats made with twelve folded bias pieces *(see page 149)*

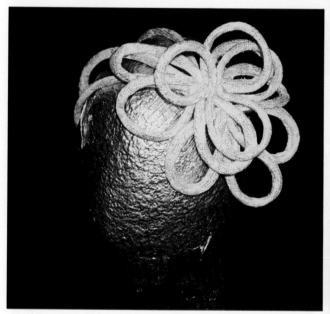

30. Six-gore navy velvet beret with suede tassels *(refer pages 47 and 129)*

31. Grey and white polyester beret; tassel made from fringing bought by the metre *(see page 129)*

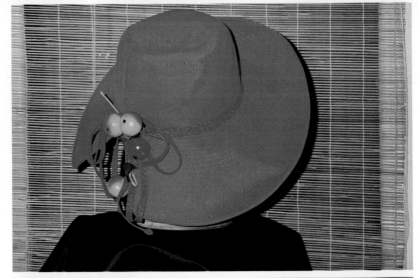

32. Red fabric hat, a simple stitched model from radii pattern, trimmed with straw and fruit *(refer page 30)*

33. Leather hat mounted on lightweight fur felt capeline, circular brim *(refer page 147)*

Cut away lace to allow ½″ (13 mm) for a collar. The brim edge is cut around the outline of the lace pattern. If this is not possible, then a small hem will be essential.

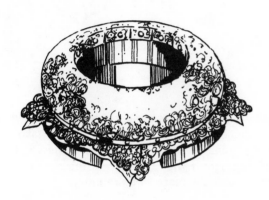

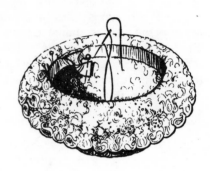

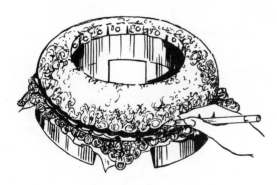

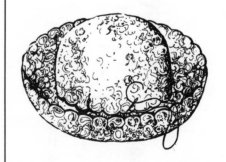

Buttonhole a wire round the inside of crown and brim. If the lace is tinted then the wire can be painted using water colour pencils. Place the crown over the collar and satin stitch round the outline of the pattern. Insert a blocked net lining and finish with a moulded ribbon head band. **Note:** If extra support is needed for a limp lace, then a cap net foundation is used.

Organdie with Crinoline Interlining

Cut bias strips of organdie and crinoline, twice the width required plus seam allowance by the amount of fabric required for the droop of brim. The less gathers the more droop. The crown is a bias strip gathered to a tip. The radius of the tip is according to taste. Baste the crinoline interlining to the wrong side of the organdie. Sew the seams on the straight grain of the fabric. Half way across these seams is the centre back. Cut away the crinoline at the seams, to the machine stitching. Press open the seams.

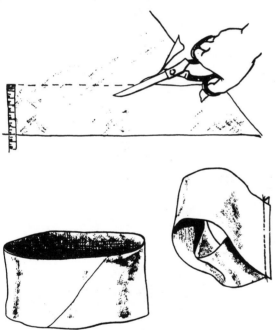

Place right side of brims to right side of crown, pin tack and machine sew. Trim away surplus fabric. Make up an organdie lining the same as the crown and sew to the headfitting. Finish with a moulded ribbon head band. **Note:** Trimming is placed before lining.

Gather the cut edges of the brims to the headfitting. Place one on top of the other and stitch. Gather the crown to the tip. Section the crown and tip into four to ensure evenness of gathers.

Wire Shape

Wire is an ideal foundation for tulle as it gives a light airy look to this fabric. It is a good support for bridal tiaras, for pearls and tulle petals. A rouleau or tubular braid threaded with wire can be moulded into interesting shapes. Always take the spring out of the wire.

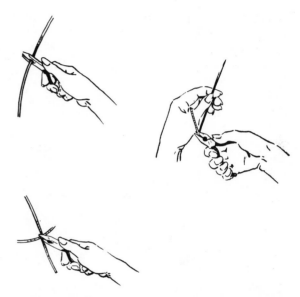

Wire will not stretch, so care must be taken to measure the wire accurately. A good overlap of 2'' (5 cm) is necessary to avoid the wire poking out. Bind the join firmly.

Several wires are used for the construction depending on the type of headdress. There is a heavy satin used for the band of a bridal tiara. Silk wire No. 24 is useful for struts or rouleau. Tie wire as the name applies is used to tie other wires together. The wire must be cleanly cut; sharp rightangle corners made where required, and the joins must be clinched together to flatten.

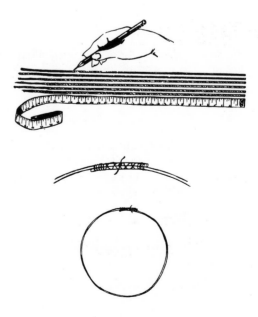

If the brim is to be made all in one with the crown, then measure off the full length from the front to back, side to side and so on, four wires in this case. When one wire has to go over another one, allow an extra length for take up. Join the wires on the crown with tie wires. Place a headfitting wire at the depth of crown and tie the struts to it.

Tie each strut with tie wire, and bend the struts over the wire. Make sure all edges of wire are facing out to avoid hurting the head. Bind the struts with folded tulle.

Bend the struts to form a brim and line the struts with a straight edge to make sure they are in line. Place an area wire for the brim edge, join it.

108

Wired Willow Extension

Construct a separate crown and brim. A brim block with the desired droop may be used. Cut and make a ½'' (13 mm) wide willow collar, and bind with bias binding, which has been ironed out. Attach this to the collar of the brim.

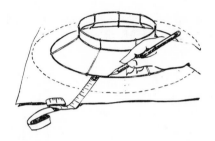

Block several layers of silk tulle or cotton net for the crown and brim. The brim may be encased with a fold of net or tulle. This is cut on the straight and merely lapped at the back, not sewn at the seam, only at the headfitting. If blocked net or tulle is used this is sewn at the brim edge and headfitting.

Place the brim on a sheet of willow, mark and cut out an extension. Wire and bind the outer edge. Fit with a bias strip of fabric, to encase the extension. Stitch the extension to the wire brim encasing the wire. Trim appropriately and line with blocked net or tulle and finish with a moulded ribbon head band.

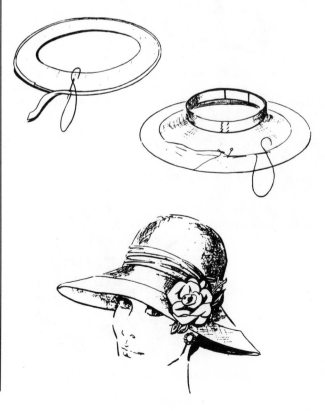

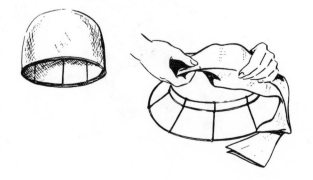

Wire Beehive

Make a shape of wire, and bind the struts with the covering fabric. Drape folds of soft fabric.

The folds can be draped in a circular direction.

Line with a blocked net lining and finish with a moulded ribbon head band.

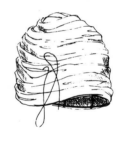

Stitch the folds to the wire, the stitches must not show. Tie stitch trimming in position.

Wire Whimsy

Cut and join bias strips of fabric, sew a cord between the folds using a zipper foot. Attach the cord at one end. Pull the other end of the cord, thus turning the rouleau to the right side. Insert millinery wire in the rouleau.

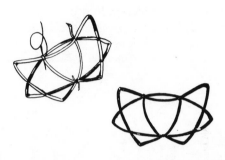

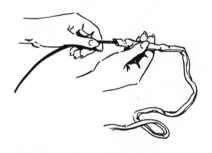

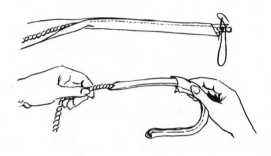

Lap and match the pattern of one yard (91 cm) of veiling. Stitch at intervals down the seam with tie stitches. Gather the top and stitch to the whimsy. Tie stitch trimming.

Mould the wired rouleau to the shape desired. Where the wires cross, stitch them together. Cut the wire a ½'' (13 mm) short of the rouleau, and finish off by twisting this over the preceding join. Stitch this in place:

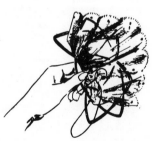

Tulle Hat

Select a sailor brim block for this hat. Make up a wire to the area edge. Place a layer of tulle top and underneath a motif of lace, feather or petals. Buttonhole the wire to the edge of the tulle. Cut into the centre to form a headfitting.

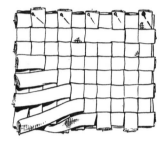

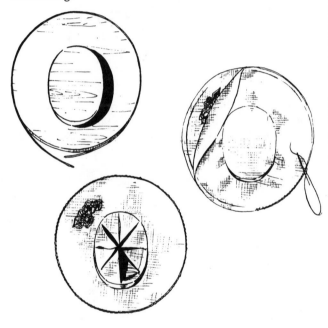

Make up a collar of willow and attach this. Bind the edge with a narrow bind. Cut lengths of tulle on the straight grain, fold them in three lengthwise, weave these and place them on a wooden block. Steam lightly. Tack around the headfitting while it is on the block to hold the folds in position.

Stiffen with felt size if necessary. Buttonhole a wire to the crown depth. Place the crown over the collar of the brim and stitch. Trim appropriately. Finish with a blocked tulle lining and moulded ribbon head band.

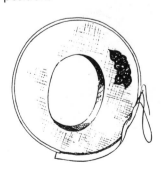

Bridal Tiara

Join a circle of satin wire to the size required. Shape silk wire No. 24 to a design. Secure wires with tie wire. Bind the wires with folded tulle.

Combs may be purchased and sewn to the sides of the tiara to hold it firmly in the air. The veil is sewn to the inside of the tiara.

Thread pearls on electrical fuse wire, and stitch with fine cotton to the bound wires.

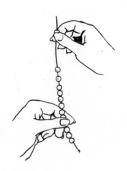

Bridal Veils

Three Tiered

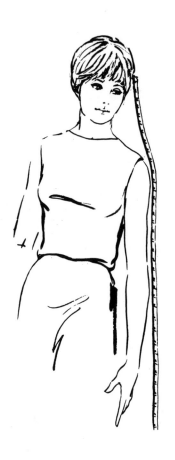

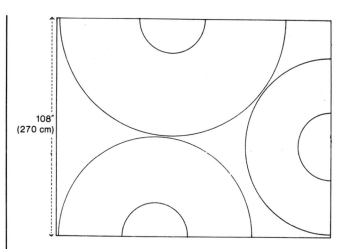

Place the three tiers together, and fold back the raw edge for a few inches to allow for a fold at the face. Have the large half circle at the headfitting a ½'' (13 mm) beyond the others, turn it over the others and stitch a running thread along the curve. Draw up the gathers and mount it to the headdress.

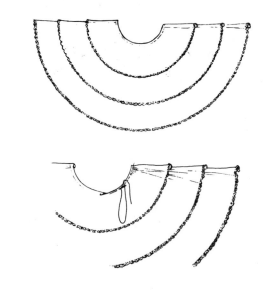

Measure the length of the veil from where the headdress will rest on the head to the bottom. 3 yards (2.75 m) of 108'' (2.75 m) wide nylon tulle or silk tulle is the usual amount for this veil. Measure the length along the edge and draw an arc of an 8'' radius. This gives enough area of net to allow it to gather for three times the measurement at the back of the head from ear to ear. Measure the length from this arc to make a half circle. Two others are cut in this way if a small detachable veil is required for the face, then a small half circle is cut in this way.

Two Circles

Two circles of tulle are cut for this veil. When measuring the bride, care must be taken to allow for a circle of 8'' (20 cm) radius, as this will be cut out to allow for gathers round the headdress. Cut two circles one larger than the other, and fold each into thirds. Cut the centre out.

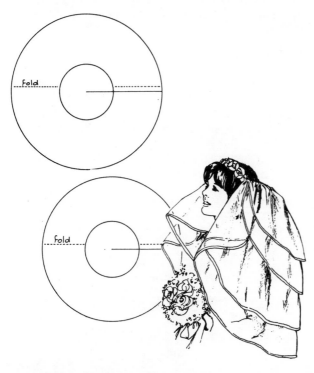

To braid the edge of a veil, an attachment may be purchased and fitted to the sewing machine in place of the ordinary foot. This is called an underbraider, and it guides the braid while it is being stitched. Paper is placed under the tulle that is to be braided to facilitate the movement of the feed dog. After the centres are cut out of the circles of tulle, a gathering thread catching the four thicknesses, and the edge is bound with fine satin.

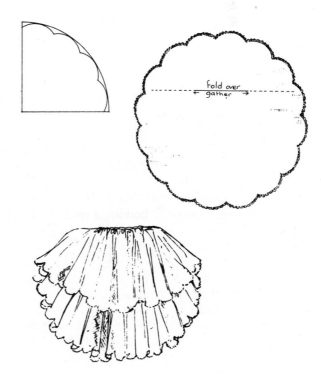

Waterfall

A waterfall veil is made from one circle. A third is folded over and a small amount of the fold is gathered. Construct a pattern by using a radius, draw a quarter of a circle, divide into equal scallops and fold into four.

Honiton Lace

Lace used for the construction of a honiton lace veil may be purchased by the metre at the lace counter at large city stores. It is a narrow lace and comes in a number of designs. For the flowers the patterns of lace are counted, allowing two for seams and the draw thread at the top allows the lace to be drawn to form a flower. The leaves are cut off in twos, but flowers may also be made with these. Very fine cotton 150 is used to stitch the flowers to the net. Broder cotton is used for the stemming.

The lace is stitched onto fine cotton net. The design is drawn onto tracing paper, one quarter of the design first, then by folding the other three quarters it can be traced off. This method ensures that the design will be equal. The design is then inked in, in indian ink. Baste the cotton net onto the other side of the paper, that has not been pencilled, otherwise the pencil will soil the net.

Working with Broder cotton, stitch the stemming first. Start where a flower will cover it. Take a stitch, then another one, the second time split the thread with the needle. Finish off the stems with this method. Joins may be covered with the application of leaves. Count off the number of patterns required in a flower, allowing two for seam. Stitch the seam, and stitch round the outline of the petals with fine cotton.

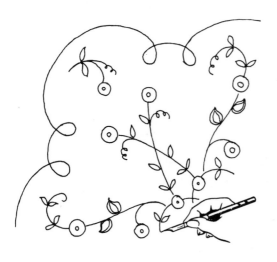

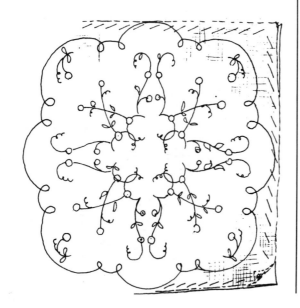

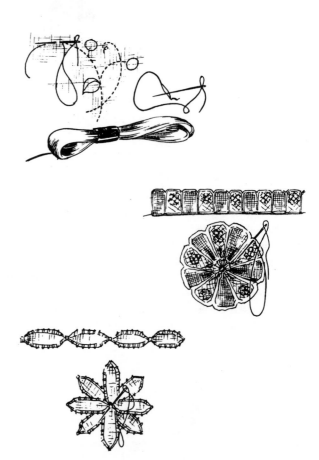

Stitch around the outline of the leaves. For the chain type of lace, stitch over the loops. For the outside edge the lace is drawn up where necessary to form scallops. Both edges of the lace are sewn to the net with fine running stitches.

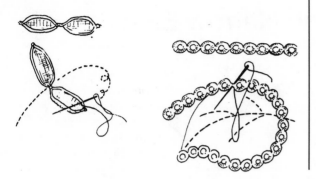

Full Stretched and Narrow Binds

Threadline 1'' (25 mm) in around brim edge. Cut a bias strip of fabric, the length of the area edge plus seam allowance by twice the width plus take up, plus seam allowance. Stretch the centre of the fabric wrong side down on the brim edge placing the pins vertically in the brim edge. Remove fabric from the brim and tack the seam. Refit the fabric to the brim edge. Machine sew the seam, press open. Place the bind in position on the brim edge, turn in the edges and slip stitch.

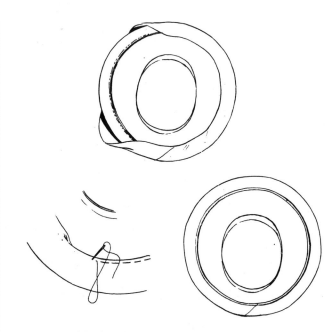

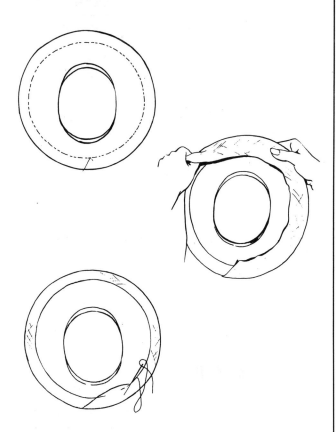

For narrow binding back stitch on edge of top of brim, turn and slip stitch. A narrow binding is made by using a narrower bias strip of fabric. This is fitted as described above, but the fabric is placed face down on the brim and back stitched on the brim edge. Turn the bias over and on the underside, turn in the raw edge and slip stitch the fold.

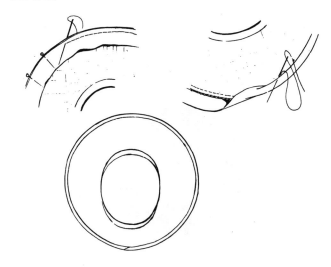

A wire may be placed under the fold of fabric, this is stitched into position with a bedding stitch. Or make up 2 wire circles to threadlined arc. Place stretched seamed bias material over. Stab stitch against wire to form a corded appearance.

Applied Scalloped Facing

The area to be scalloped is marked off on a foundation of willow, canvas or vilene. Make a pattern to the required design and transfer this to the foundation. Cut away surplus fabric, and stitch the two raw edges together on the wrong side. If using a heavy fabric, it may be glued to the foundation.

Slip stitch the outer edge to the brim. If a design is required for a crown then a radius shape with a seam at the centre back would be used.

Ruched Ribbon

Join a wire to the dimensions of the area edge of the brim. Fold a ribbon into thirds over this wire and using a stab stitch, push the ribbon along the wire and so gather and stitch in the one operation. Stitch the ribbon facing to the under brim.

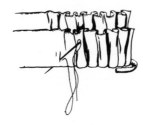

Bias Folds

Plain Pleated Facing

Cut fabric on the true bias, twice the width required plus seam allowance. This can be used in a variety of ways on brims and crowns. A light foundation is all that is required.

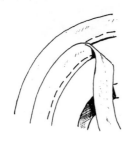

For a pleated facing, mark off 1'' (25 mm) squares on paper. This pleating takes a little more than three times the fabric for the area edge. Cut a bias strip of fabric the width required plus seam allowance by the length. Baste the fabric to the paper, and pick up the dots 1'' (25 mm) apart for three rows. Remove fabric from the paper and pleat.

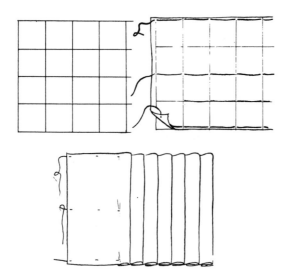

Place the pleated fabric on the brim to be covered and position the pleats. To make a join do not sew a seam, merely lap the pleats. Turn the seam allowance over the edge and diagonally baste. This method of pleating is suitable for transparent fabrics.

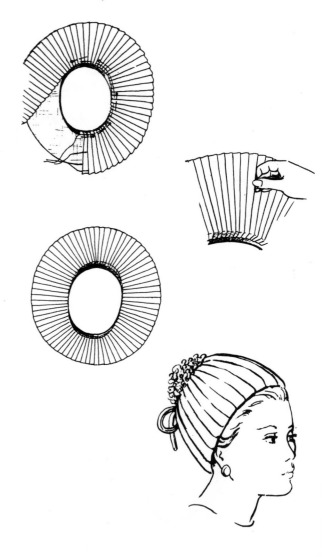

Fancy Facing

Cut bias strips of fabric twice the width required plus seam allowance. Fold in halves.

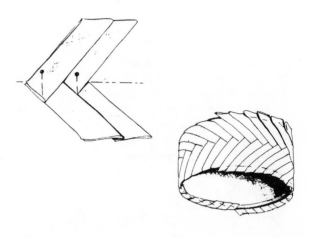

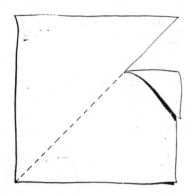

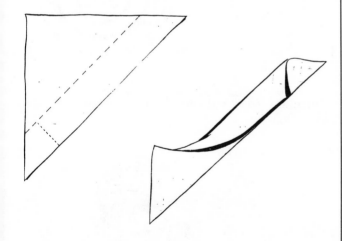

Make a crown or brim foundation and threadline the centre. Place the folded bias strips at right angles to each other. Place these on the threadline, with the centre of the rightangle touching the threadline. Stitch with a running stitch.

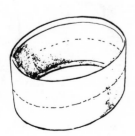

Turn the ends over the edge of the frame and diagonally baste.

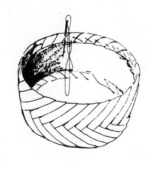

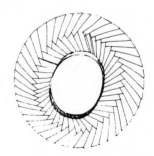

Puffed Extension

Cut a bias strip of fabric one and a half to three times the size of the area to be covered plus seam allowance. Machine the seam and press open. Divide this circle and the area to be covered in four. Mark with a thread. Threadline the area for the finished extension. Place gathering threads on each edge, and encasing the edge of the brim with the extension, match the four marked sections and draw up the threads.

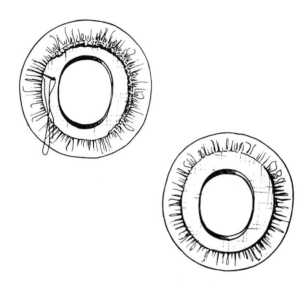

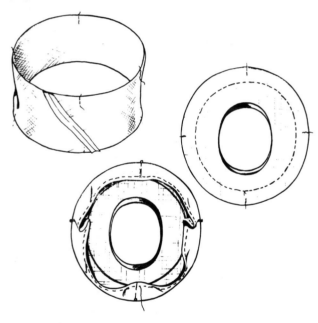

Place circles of wire on the threadlines and fold the gathered fabric over them, pin and stab stitch between the folds.

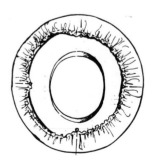

There are many and varied ways of using the puffed extension.

Millinery Bows

Millinery bows are made in a great number of shapes and sizes. They may be made of silk ribbon of an immense variety of kinds and widths, nylon and velvet ribbon, lace, piece velvet, chiffon, tulle, straw, kid, braid, fur, cloth, etc., but each bow is made on the same general principle. Before using new ribbon, it is better for an inexperienced worker to practise on a piece of muslin, or even tissue paper, cut in strips the width and length of the ribbon; for when once the ribbon is creased, it cannot very well be altered without taking away the freshness of its appearance. By practising this way, the beginner will obtain that lightness of touch, quickness and 'finger-knack' which is so necessary in all millinery trimmings, and especially in bow-making. The student will, in a short time, produce bows which would be a credit to an experienced milliner.

Bows are always made by hand before they are sewn on. When making the bow, the hat for which the ribbon is needed should be in front of the worker, to obtain the size and effect.

Bows are best made from one length of ribbon which is not cut more than necessary, unless a bow with many ends is required.

A bow although it would appear untouched by hand, must yet be firm. When buying ribbons for bows take care that the assistant does not crease the ribbon to show how it will look, as the crease may happen to come across the widest part of the loop. The following characteristics of a well-made bow should be noted:

Pleats should be even, fine and straight.
Each loop and end brought back to its root and starting point, and the bow made in one piece, if possible.
The ribbon kept fresh-looking, and free from any re-arrangements.
The size of the loops made in accordance with the width of the ribbon.
Wire (if used) firmly fixed, and the ribbon sewn lightly to it, free from strain.

First make a few bows which are always fashionable. The quantity of material required for a simple bow is ¾ yd. (69 cm) of 4″ (10 cm) wide ribbon.

Start at one end not in the centre. Hold the ribbon in the right hand and with the left, pleat it firmly and evenly. Bind it tightly round the pleats with cotton, using a 'straw' needle and cotton. Insert the needle once through the pleats and turn the cotton round tightly three times; put the needle through again (a).

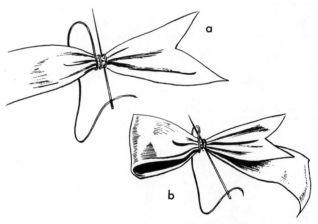

Gauge the length of the loop by the width of the ribbon—the wider the ribbon the longer loops. Pleat the ribbon evenly and bring the pleated part back to the centre, and bind it tightly with the cotton, having the loop opposite the end just made (b). This centre is called the root or waist of the bow.

Make a loop in the opposite direction, which will place it on the top of the first end, and for this simple bow make it the same length as the first loop, bringing it back to the root or starting point. Cut off the ends slatways, or fray them out. The triangular cut from the first end will make the tie-over. Turn in the cut edges, twist it over the root, and neatly finish off at the back with a few stitches (c).

If there is a right and wrong side to the ribbon, as there is in velvet ribbon with satin back and most ribbons with patterns in them, give it a sharp twist to keep the right side up, before making the second loop. To pull up the loop, place the forefinger inside. Never crease or touch bows more than is necessary to secure them.

On this principle all other bows are made. They may be varied by having several loops of different lengths, but they are always placed alternately right and left to the root.

A butterfly bow (d) has two loops and two upstanding ends, shaped at the ends as butterfly wings. It makes a handsome trimming if made of wide ribbon, or a piece of silk. Start this time with a loop, pleating each side separately. Make another loop in the opposite direction, then another standing up in the centre, turning in the end inside, passing the cotton used to secure the bow at the root through and through the loop. Pass the tie through the centre loop. Cut this slantways (e) and shape the ends like butterfly wings. Quantity of ribbon required is ⅝ yard (57 cm) of 2 inch (5 cm) wide ribbon.

A tied bow (f) has as many loops of various sizes as desired, but only two ends, and is made including the tie-over in one piece. It is useful for children's washing hats as well as other millinery. Keep the first and second loop the longest, graduating the length of each pair of loops. Begin with an end, next a loop 12″ (30 cm) long, in opposite direction, another loop the same length as the first 12″ (30 cm) long, then two loops 9″ (22.5 cm) long and two loops 6″ (15 cm) long. Take the remainder of the ribbon, twist it around the root, and pull the end through the twist at the back, and the bow is finished.

This bow can be made without the use of any cotton; the loops are kept firmly in place with the fingers till the tie-over is reached, that is the second end. Quantity of ribbon required is 2¼ yards (2 m) 4″ (10 cm) wide.

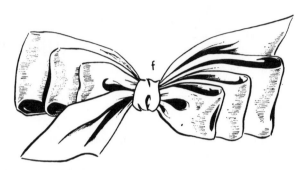

The Alsatian bow (g) takes 1¼ yards (1.15 m) of 3″ (7.5 cm) wide ribbon. It is made of four loops, has no ends, and a large broad tie-over. Loops Nos. 1 and 2 are 12″ (30 cm) long, loops 3 and 4 are 10″ (25 cm) long. This bow has only one pleat in the centre. The loops are made flat and before the tie over is placed the ribbon is pleated. Fold a tie over the centre.

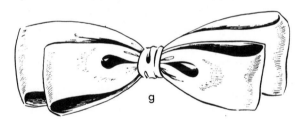

Fancy bows with more than two ends, and more than two or four loops, are made on the same principle described, several of the loops being cut after the bow is made. If an upstanding end is required, the tie-over is taken around them, and for a flatter trimming, the tie-over is taken in the centre in the usual way.

Ends of bows may be frayed, cut in wing, mitred, or cut to fishtail shapes. The ends are sometimes vandyked, or treated in some other fashion.

Kilting the ribbon makes pretty, effective bows. Plain ribbon looks better kilted than fancy ribbons. Mixing ribbons of different tones of the same colour makes smart bows. Good French ribbons are easy to match in this way; graduating the colour from light to dark.

Piece velvet bows are made of velvet cut on the bias and the edges rolled hemmed. The loops are pleated as in ribbon bows; but as velvet is much thicker, it should be twisted as little as possible, and if a large bow is required, it must be made in two parts. About ¾ yard (69 cm) on the bias is required, and the tie-over should be neatly made.

Bows of straw, braid, etc., are made in the same way.

Lace insertion sewn between the rows of straw. Two or even three colours of straw worked in one bow is also very effective.

In stitching bows to the hat, stitch firmly, stabbing the needle in the hat through the back part of the bow tie-over. Tie inside. Catch each loop to the brim with an invisible tie-stitch in a becoming position. That is it should be placed to follow the 'line' of the hat. It is also better to keep the one 'feature', for example, if a hat has a fold, pleat, or flute, then this is the place to arrange the bow or trimming.

Trimming a hat is most important and when choosing a bow, keep in mind style, texture, quality, colour, line and balance.

The style must be in keeping with the type of hat, for example a severely tailored 'suit' hat would require a tailored bow.

Contrast in texture is required, and this can be obtained by using satin, grosgrain, velvet, nylon ribbon, or fabric (stitched). Then again the contrast in texture must harmonise with the style of hat. Quality is important and a cheap satin ribbon can mar an elegant hat.

Colour must be carefully chosen and care must be taken to tone or contrast the trimming. If a trimming to tone is decided, for example, if the hat is red-brown, then a ribbon of a lighter tone, or darker shade with a suggestion of red is required. Be careful not to choose a colour that is too far removed. Consult the colour wheel if you are in doubt.

Proportion the bow to the hat and make sure it balances. If you wish to use narrow velvet ribbon, and the hat obviously requires a large bow, then it is essential to use three narrow bows to obtain balance. An odd number looks better than an even number.

When the ends of the ribbon are required to stand up, they need to be wired. Ribbon wire is used, just single strands, and it is lightly stitched to the centre of the ribbon or the sides.

Good ribbons require no stiffening, provided the loops are not too long. Large bows of wide ribbon, and all soft ribbons, require wiring. Use ribbon wire, shredded. Use each strand of the wire separately, which can easily be done by tearing it along the soft part. Buttonhole stitch it along the centre, and zig-zag the wire for wider softer ribbons. Use a very fine sewing silk to match the ribbon, and let the stitch taken through be hardly visible.

Upstanding or broad ends should be wired half way up, never quite to the top. The ends are wired one, or both sides of the ribbon, as the case may be.

Ribbon Bows

Cut two lengths of ribbon. The shorter one has the ends fish-tailed and the folds of the longer portion just meet the angle of the fishtail. These are stitched in the centre. The tie-over has the edges folded inwards. Pleat the centre of the ribbon and stitch the tie over at the back.

Mitre the ends in opposite directions for this bow. A flat tie over is used.

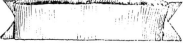

Cut two lengths and fishtail the ends. Fold tie over into thirds and place this over the ribbon, stitch at the back.

Fold a length of ribbon in halves and place a tie-over a third of the distance from the fold on the pleated ribbon.

The tie-over on this bow has the edges folded inwards on the right side.

Ribbon Trims

Fold the ribbon at right angles alternately. Fold the two triangles together, then fold another rightangle and place this triangle to the one just made.

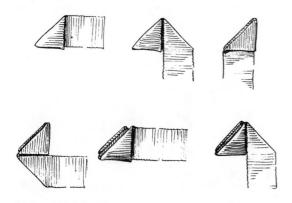

Make box pleats and catch the edges together or turn the folds at rightangles.

Continue in this way until enough folds are made to form a circle. Tuck the end into the fold. Stitch the points together. To form a ball, stitch both top and base points. Stitch to a pleated and mitred length of ribbon.

Place the forefinger under the ribbon and twist to form a triangle. Make several triangles and roll to form a ball or a barrel shape.

Pleat the ribbon evenly and fold the corners at rightangles.

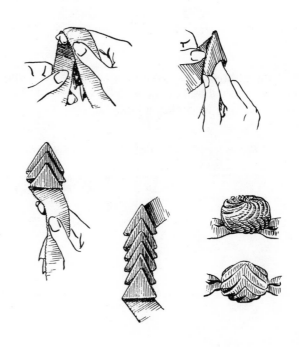

Fold the ribbon at rightangles to form a triangle. With the ribbon on the right hand side form another triangle. Turn this triangle under and up.

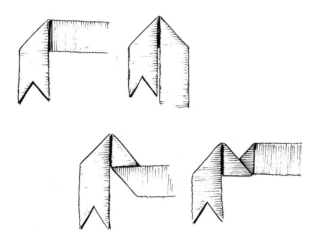

Continue as described above to form a trim. Conceal stitches in the folds.

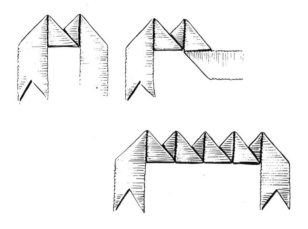

Fold the ribbon at rightangles until a square is formed. Make three squares. Fringe the end of a length of ribbon, roll and attach to centre of box.

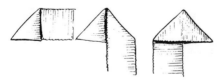

Mark off a length of ribbon at ½" (12 mm) intervals, and pleat to form 24 pleats. Sew the pleats round a buckram base. Gather a section of ribbon and sew into the centre. Mitre the ends of a length of ribbon, fold in halves, pleat and place in the centre of the gathers.

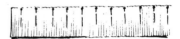

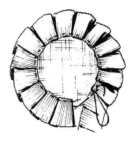

Tassels

Cut a piece of grosgrain fabric 9'' (23 cm) wide, by 6'' (15 cm) long, or nine pieces of grosgrain ribbon 1'' (25 mm) wide and 6'' (15 cm) long. Fray the fabric by pulling the threads from the base, leaving 1'' (25 mm) at the top. Roll the fabric to form a cylinder.

Select a length of felt and make several cuts along each edge. Roll the felt. Place around the centre of the roll a narrow length of felt. Tie off each end and place a pearl in each knot.

Take hold of the 1'' (25 mm) section and completely turn the threads over the unfrayed section. Bind the throat with several of the threads. Buttonhole a loop of the thread and stitch the loop into position.

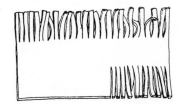

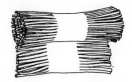

Cubist Rose

Cut 4 large and 4 smaller squares of fabric, e.g. 8'' × 8'' (20 × 20 cm) and 6'' × 6'' (15 × 15 cm) and fold these over to form a triangle. Place the small sections one on top of the other alternately with the folded edges facing inwardly.

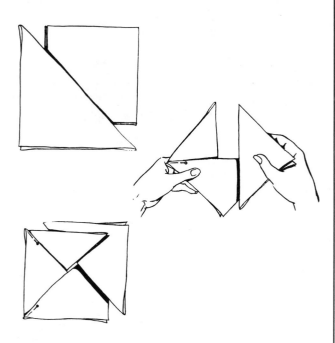

Gather round the outside edge. Draw up to form a ball, leave the cotton and needle attached. This is the centre.

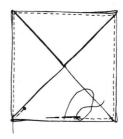

Turn back the corners of the larger triangles, and place these as for the smaller ones.

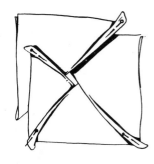

Gather the base. Place the centre into the outer petals and stitch. Make and place leaves in position. Cover the base with a circle of fabric to neaten.

Cabochon Rose

For the base, cut a circle of willow the desired size, and dart this to form a conical shape. Wire and bias bind the edge. Cover this with an interlining.

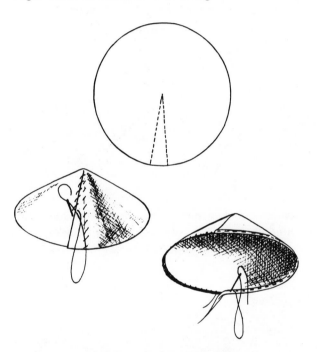

Cut bias strips of fabric, and fold these in half; link these as in a chain. Pin and sew these to the shape. Place another bias strip across these, allowing enough slack to give a natural shape, to represent a rose petal.

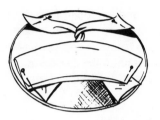

Arrange more bias strips around the shape, alternating them to give the appearance of a rose. The last strips need to be cut wider to allow them to be turned under the shape and diagonally basted. Use a darker fabric for the centre.

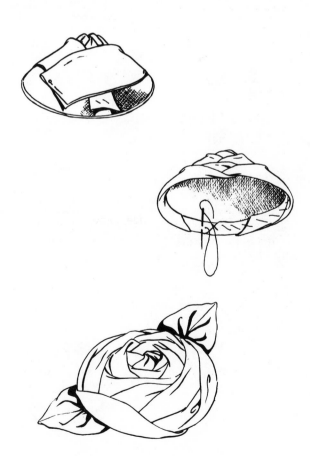

Bias Roses

Cut several strips of bias fabric of different lengths; mitre the ends. Fold the fabric in halves lengthwise, and place a gathering stitch round the edge. Draw the cotton to form gathers. The tighter the gathers are drawn the wider the rose opens at that section. To form a bud, roll a small section tightly.

A rose may be made with just one length of fabric. This is mitred at the end and gathered in the same way. Starting the bud with very little gather, as the rose is required to open gather more in that section.

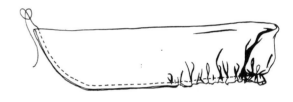

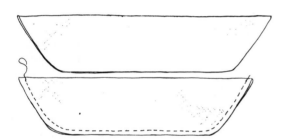

Continue encircling the bud with the fold and finish with a mitred corner at the base, leaves may be added. Cut a small circle of fabric and stitch this to the base to neaten it.

Place the remaining gathered folds alternately round the bud. Don't start the next one where the last one finished. Continue to add the folds until the desired size is achieved.

Briar Rose

Cut a square of fabric and fold it in halves. Gather round the cut edges and draw them up to form a petal.

Place a wire over the centre of a group of stamens. Fold the petals round the wired stamens, placing them alternately. Secure the petals with a few stitches.

Place some leaves in position, stitch them and finish with a circle of fabric.

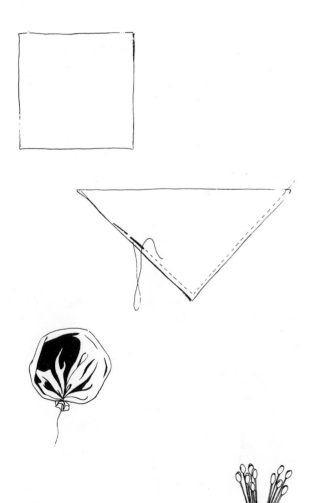

Tulle and Organza Petals

These petals are suitable to use in conjunction with a bridal headdress. Pearl stamens add glamour to these. Cut a small square of tulle approximately 4½'' (11 cm). Fold this diagonally. Mould a length of 22 gauge fuse wire round a paste bottle; twist the wire to secure and shape it to form a leaf.

Another petal may be made with lightweight fabric. This is a square folded diagonally over a length of fuse wire, for a short distance.

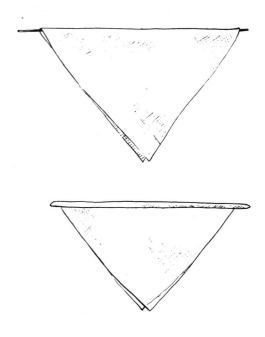

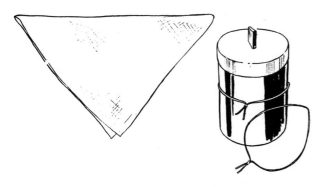

Bring the ends of the wire together, gathering the fabric. Tie cotton round the base.

Place the wire inside the fold of tulle and gather it to the base. Tie off with cotton.

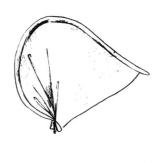

Leaves

Use a natural leaf, and cut a shape in willow. Buttonhole a wire round the edge, and fold the bias binding, which has been ironed flat over the edge and stab stitch it. Place a piece of fabric on one side; fold the edges over the binding, and diagonally baste. For the other side turn the raw edges under and slip stitch. This leaf is attractive beaded, and a small pillbox is attractive covered with them.

A piece of hat felt may be cut to a leaf shape and stitched in continuous circles starting from the centre. A most attractive leaf or petal is this one which is cut from a long piece of fabric on the bias. The fabric is folded in halves lengthwise, wrong sides facing, then in halves again so that there are four raw edges together. Stitch from the fold to the base, curving off the points. Trim the surplus fabric away and open out at the fold. On the right stitch down right side of the centre, catching the seam at the back to flatten it. An interlining of linen canvas gives a moulded effect. A small hat is elegant made of these leaves. A wire shape could serve as a base.

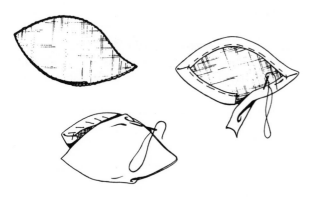

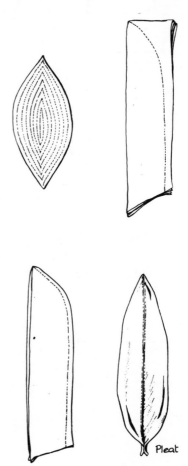

Outline a leaf pattern on two pieces of fabric, the right sides facing, either machine stitch round all the way and cut a slit in the back to turn through, or nearly all the way, and turn through the small opening. The edges are turned and slip stitched. Of course the seam allowance must be trimmed before turning through and the points cut off. Machine stitch veins on the right side.

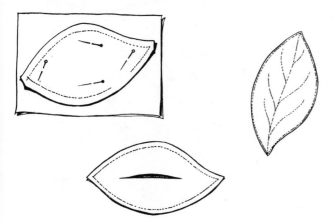

Cut an oblong of fabric, fold it in halves and stitch, starting from the fold on one side. Turn it through to the right side and open it out to form a triangle. Alternately pleat the base starting at the centre.

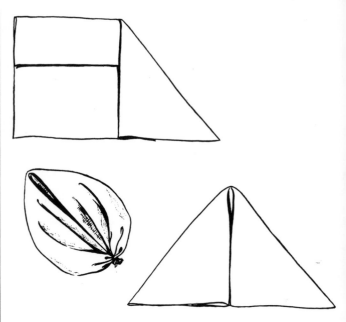

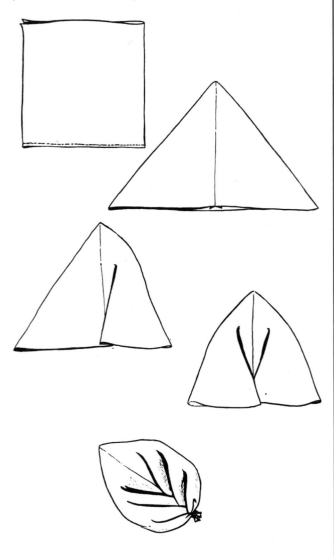

Organandie leaves

Cut a leaf shape in organdie, on the bias. Moistening start at the top and roll the organdie between the forefinger and thumb. Then roll the other side. This leaf requires some practice.

This leaf may be made from fabric or ribbon; cut an oblong of fabric or ribbon, fold one edge towards the centre for a third of the distance. Turn the folds towards the centre to form a triangle and pleat.

Flowers and Fruit

Tulip

Stiffen some fabric, e.g. straw cloth with straw stiffener. Use the pattern illustrated and cut six petals on the bias of the fabric. Pleat the base of each and place them alternately round a rouleau that has been strengthened with wire. The petals are glued and tied with cotton individually.

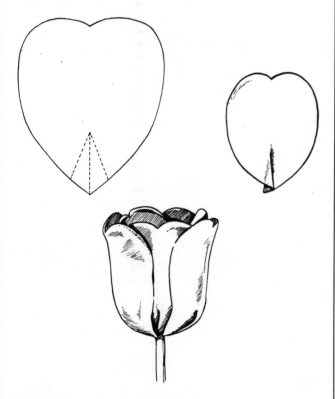

Apple

Cut a circle of fabric, e.g. green silk, the size the apple is required. Wind a length of flower making wire round the centre of a piece of cottonwool. Cut a circle of cottonwool and fold this round the centre just made; tie the base with cotton. Place a gathering thread round the fabric circle and draw this round the base, tie off the cotton.

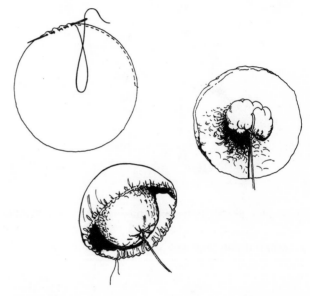

Attach a clove to a thread and attach it to the base of the apple. The apple may be tinted by mixing aniline dye with methylated spirits. It is a good idea to copy a natural one.

Pad the wire with cottonwool and bind it with brown crepe paper. Leaves may be made as illustrated for the tooled leaves.

Grapes

These are oval in shape. Therefore make this shape using cotton wool and paste. Place a wire round the centre and twist it to tighten. Gather a circle of fabric to cover the shape. Tie the cotton at the base.

Twist a length of green flowermaking wire round a pencil and use these as tendrils. Make a leaf and group this with an odd number of grapes and a few tendrils together. Tie them and bind the stem.

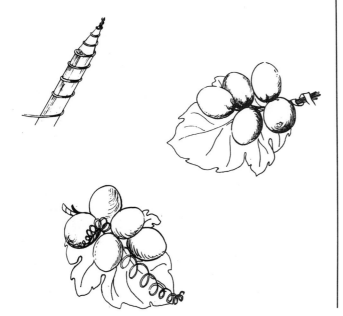

Cherries

Make a ball of cotton wool over a hooked wire. Gather a circle of fabric over this, tie the cotton and trim it. Make a group of these, also a leaf. Attach them to a padded and bound wire. Try and copy the colouring of the natural fruit.

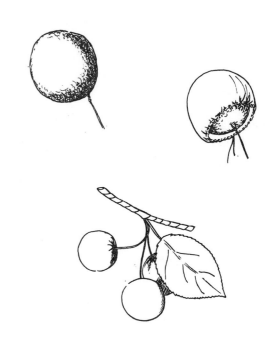

Tooled Flowers

The method known as tooled, or french flowers is one by which the petals are cut to the shape of the flowers and are tooled with a hot instrument that may be purchased at hobby stores. These stores also have a vast range of stamens, wires, leaves, crepe paper, stemming, dyes, tools, glue and other requirements for flower making.

Necessary requirements for this type of flower making are the following:

A plastic sheet to keep the table clean
A set of tools
Beeswax to clean the tools
A methylated spirit lamp
Methylated spirits
A rubber mat or a sand cushion (a bag filled with sand)
Aniline dyes
Material stiffener
Several small paint brushes
Small bowls for mixing dyes
Glue and paste
Small scissors

Such fabrics as lawn, organdie, silk, satin, taffeta or velvet, the latter has a special stiffener. These fabrics are best in white and dyed to obtain a more realistic effect. If the primary colour dyes are purchased, these can be mixed to copy nature.

Stamens
Leaf fabric, crepe paper or stemming
Wire for flower making

When making these flowers, natural results are obtained by picking a live flower from the garden and pulling it to pieces to obtain the patterns and to copy the colouring. The fabric is stiffened with material stiffener allowed to dry. The pattern is outlined with pencil on the wrong side of the fabric and carefully cut out. The petal is first dipped in methylated spirit then in aniline dye which has been mixed with methylated spirit in a tone to represent the colour of the flower to be made. If the petal is darker at the base or is another colour then this is applied with a small paint brush. Allow the dyed petals to dry.

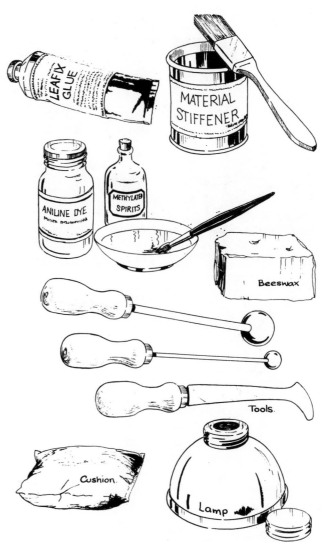

Tool the petals with the appropriate tools, the natural flower will indicate this, e.g. a round tool to cup a rose petal, a knife tool to mark a daisy, or a small round tool to curl a chrysanthemum.

The leaves are cut out after they are glued to the backing fabric, then tooled. The flower is finished with a calyx and the wire stem is covered with crepe paper or stemming. The stem if necessary may be padded with cotton wool.

Chrysanthemum

Stiffen white fabric e.g. lawn and organdie with material stiffener, if using velvet this requires a special stiffener. Trace the patterns illustrated on page 00 that is if a natural flower is not available. Place the patterns on the bias of the fabric and pencil round the outline.

Using small scissors carefully cut round the outline. The petals may need to be cut deeper. Any number of petals may be cut, according to the size of the flower required.

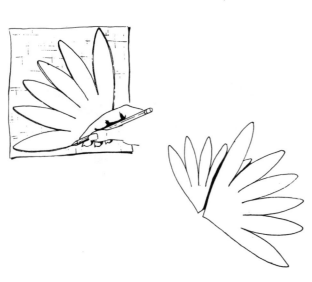

Using tweezers, dip the petals in methylated spirits, and while they are still wet, mix some aniline dye with methylated spirits in the appropriate colour and paint this on the petal. A darker shade may be run in from the base. The petal must be damp otherwise a hard line will result. Allow the petals to dry before tooling.

For the chrysanthemum heat a small ball tool.

Rub the tool in beeswax to clean it, then heat it again. Place the petal on a sand bag cushion or covered rubber mat and starting at the tip, drag the tool down the petal, pressing firmly. Turn the petal over and tool the next serration in the same manner. Tool all the petals alternately like this.

Bend a length of wire to form a hook. Glue the base of a small petal and apply it to the base of the wire. Tie the base of the petal with cotton. Attach the petals in this way, placing them round the wire, until the size of the flower that is required is obtained. Place several darker tinted petals first then the larger lighter toned ones. Care must be taken to keep the petals level and not to let them run down the stem. It is always advisable to copy from a natural flower for best results.

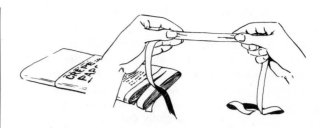

Mitre the corner, and place a small amount of glue on the end. Place this point to the base of the flower and twist it round the stem. Leaves may be added during this process. A little colour run into the stem is effective.

Cut a calyx, and cut a cross in the centre. Glue this to the base of the flower. Cut a length of crepe paper a ½'' (12 mm) wide; take the stretch out of it.

Daisy

It is a good idea to pick flowers from the garden and obtain patterns and colouring from them. For the daisy, stiffen the fabric with material stiffener and cut out the pattern, cutting down towards the centre to separate the petals. Cut a cross in the base of a group of petals.

Heat the knife tool and tool in the centre on the wrong side and down each side on the right side of each petal. Make a centre for the daisy by winding wool round a piece of cardboard. Tie off the base and cut the threads at the top.

Place a wire through the loops and twist off to fasten. Trim the wool and brush with a wire brush to matt the fibres. Place some glue at the base and thread the wire through the cross cut in the group of petals. Place two groups of petals, alternating them. Bind the stem with crepe paper. Place leaves in position.

Place wire at bottom of folded cardboard and wind wool round

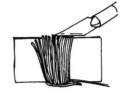

Bend wire to secure wool and cut wool between cardboard at top

When possible a flower from the garden could be used

Tighten wire and brush wool with wire brush

Stiffen material pencil round pattern and cut as previously shown

Slip daisy petals up to wool centre glue and bind with cotton

Tool down centre back of petals

Finish daisy stem with paper

Rose

Make a centre for the rose by folding a piece of cottonwool over a hooked wire, and moulding it into shape using paste and shaping with the fingers. Cut and tint several rose petals, it will be noticed that most flowers are usually darker in the centre. Tool the petals in the centre, by selecting a tool appropriate to the size of petal to be tooled. Press into the centre of the petal so making it a cup shape as it is in reality.

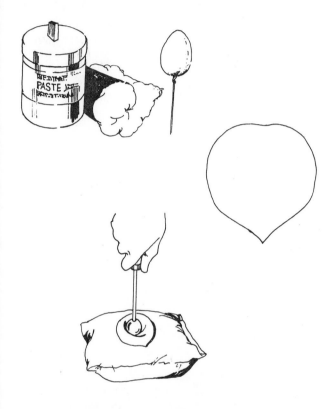

Most rose petals are curled outwards, so this is done by using a pronged tool or a knitting needle. Heat the tool and wrap the edge of the petal round it. Glue the base of the petal and cup it round the centre. Tie with strong cotton. Place the petals alternately round the bud glueing and tying until the rose is the desired size.

Glue a calyx in position, and cut a strip of crepe paper, mitre the end and wind this round the stem. Place glue at either end to secure. Leaves are placed as desired. A better job is obtained if a natural flower is copied in the process of making, as memory cannot be relied upon.

Tooled Leaves

Apply glue to the wrong side of a piece of leaf fabric. Place wire in position and place a piece of crepe paper on top. Outline the edge of the leaf using if possible a natural leaf. Cut round outline, tool down the centre either side of the wire and mark veining, copying the natural leaf.

Rose calyx

Stiffen material and glue two pieces together with wire between

Rose leaf

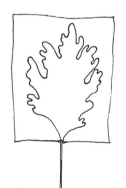

Pencil round pattern and cut out

Chrysanthemum leaf

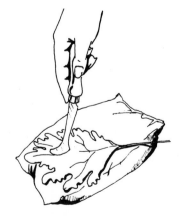

Tool veins in leaf and finish by binding the stem with paper on wire

Daisy leaf

Petal Patterns

For the rose cut several petals of all sizes the size depending on of rose to be made.

Chrysanthemum petals are in three sizes and the size of flower required will indicate the number of petals to cut.

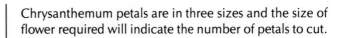

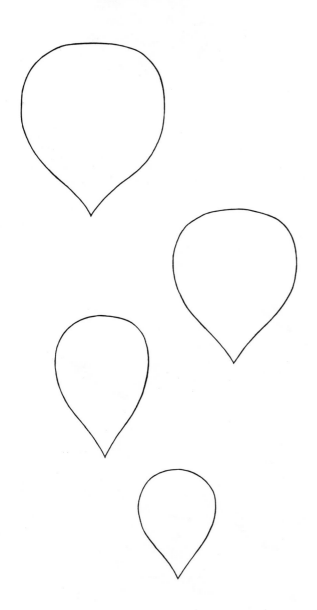

Daisy patterns, cut two.

Feather Trims

Select feather pads in the tonings required. Cut out a shape in buckram. Glue a pad to the tail portion and shape this by cutting the feathers. Place and glue another pad in position at the head. Sew a spangle, with a seed bead in the centre of it, to the feather and through the buckram to represent the eye.

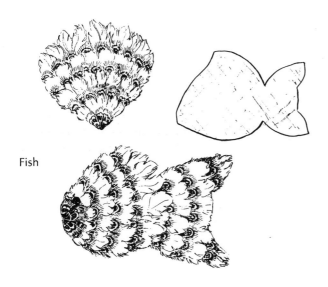

Fish

A butterfly is made from two feather pads. The antenna and body is rouleau threaded with wire. The head is made with a few tiny feathers glued in position.

For a pheasant, place two feathers one on top of the other; these are the looser type. Make a body from cotton wool with a wire or portion of feather protruding for a beak. Cover the wire with crepe paper, glue in position. Glue some small feathers to the cotton wool body.

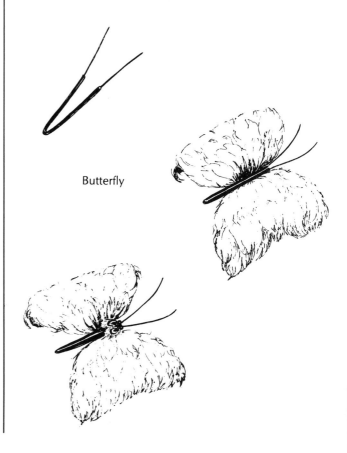

Butterfly

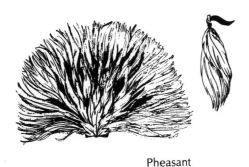

Pheasant

Fur, Leather and Imitation Leather or Vynex Hats

Fur hats are made from selected pelts. When making a fur hat, it is advisable to construct a pattern with a ½'' (12 mm) roll over on the headfitting edge of the crown and the outer edge of the brim. Consult a furrier, as he will advise as to the selection of pelts for the type of hat required.

The cutting, sewing and making of the pelts is a very specialised trade, pelts like mink stretch under inexperienced hands. The fur must run to or from a central point; the pelts must be matched for colour.

The lightweight furs such as mink are mounted on willow, and the heavier type for example, Belini Lamb, Fez would be mounted on vilene. The heavy type has its own hide to support. The furrier will leave a tape on the edge of the brim or crown to allow for attaching to the support.

Furs are usually lined with a good quality satin to match the richness. If the fur requires a trim then a shiny fabric makes a suitable contrast.

Leather hats are made from the skin or hide of the animal, if the hide is thick, the edges that are to be sewn need to be pared away to make them fine enough to sew. This is done with a skiving knife, which is a wide sharp blade attached to a handle and is used with a half circular motion, pushing away from the body.

Suede, glove leather or vynex are not skived.

To sew the leather or vynex, a bayonet pointed needle is used, or a very thick needle. Thick cotton No. 36 is required. The sewing machine is set for a longer stitch, the tensions and pressure should be adjusted. A special attachment can be purchased for the machine and it is called a walking foot. It is excellent for sewing leather and vynex.

Instructions for Making Hats in Colour Plates

Plate 1. Satin hat trimmed with veiling and soft silk flowers. Elliptical brim, wide sides, narrow front and narrower still at back; brim placed on top of crown. Good for a mother-of-the-bride as the brim is up off the face. Made with Leno. Brim padded with Vilene and machine stitched underneath. Use adhesive for top. Crown of Leno padded with foam, and satin pulled firmly over. Three little pleats may be needed each side.

Plate 2. Shaded green chiffon hat mounted in three layers on stiff matching veiling. Wet veil and chiffon and pull down over crown. For the brim stitch three layers of veil together, machining in circles. Attach bottom, then top with the chiffon by spraying with fast drying adhesive spray. Bias double band around the crown and edge. Trim with cubist roses and silk leaves with a wire down the centre. (Refer pages 101 – brim; 102 – crown; 112 – tulle brim; 120 – pleated folds; 130 – cubist rose.)

Plate 3. Milan straw model with satin crown mounted on a Leno shape. Satin edge and bows.

Plate 4. Pink Thai silk on Leno or Sparterie. Mould crown; cover with layer of cotton wool. Wet silk and pull over same block. Leave to dry, then place over padded crown. Make brim required width and shape. Machine stitch top layer to Leno. Spray underneath with fast drying adhesive, pat into shape; wire edge and cover with muslin. Stitch 4'' (10 cm) bias onto top side, pulling firmly. Make a bias join at back by machine. Feather is of material cut to shape, turned, and a rouleau with wire down the centre. (Refer page 24.)

Plate 5. Two fur felt sailor hats made from capelines. *Light grey hat:* wired around the outside edge; cover with petersham ribbon. Band shaped around crown to be absolutely flat. Use tissue paper, cut to a width of about 3'' (7.5 cm), and shape with tiny pleats. Cut interlining; lie it face down on back of trimming which is cut wider to fold over. Then glue lightly. *Green hat:* trim with bias velvet. (Refer page 18.)

Plate 6. Fine green wool hat trimmed with green satin cut in bias. Flower petals cream underneath. Machine stitch centre of petals and leave enough room to push up a piece of wire to give them a lift. Centre made of narrow folded loops. Leno crown covered with foam, then fine Vilene glued to each side for padding. Start machining on outside edge, going round and round in a continuous line. This picture shows the bias join at the back. If short of material make two joins either side of back.

Plate 7. Black hat with ostrich feather trim. Make a fairly shallow crown to fit the head. Wire edge and put bias around this as a trim. Make crown wider on the right down side, narrow in front, and narrower still at the back. The centre hole is large enough to come to the bottom edge of the crown, low on right side and up a little on the left, enough to carry a bow or flowers; up at back.

Plate 9. Six sectioned crown sports hat in red denim. The crown can be dinted or folded for variation. (Refer pages 55–56.)

Plate 10. White straw braid with 2'' (25 mm) petersham trim. Brim is wired onto shape covered with narrow bias binding made from shapewell or muslin. Fold petersham in two and curve, then machine. It takes a little practice to get both edges stitched close to edge. (Refer page 78.)

Plate 11. *Pink breton:* pulled up sharply off the face. (Refer pages 71–72.)
Tan straw hat: Shaped up a little all round with extra height on right side. This is done with the fingers, and pulled in a little, with wire on the edge.

Plate 12. Paribuntal straw capeline trimmed with good quality satin. Cut binding for edge 3'–4'' wide (7.5–10 cm) on the bias. Swathed trim is cut with one smaller piece for the bottom. Stitch folds on top. (Refer to page 70; page 118 for bias.)

Plate 13. Cocktail or mother-of-the-bride hats.
(a) Blue satin over padded Leno. Bias cuff stitched onto crown then turned up. Loops at the back lined with tulle and not pressed. A few rouleau loops at lower back—thread with thick string and pull cover tight, when they will circle into shapes.
(b) Shape as above. Trim with crinoline. Make flowers by pulling the cotton edge firmly; the crinoline will then curl into shape.
(c) Sheer material over green interlining.

Plate 14. Black satin crown with see-through brim. Make crown of Leno or Sparterie, cut fairly deep at back, and cover with padding. Cover tip with satin and pull down until little pleats start to appear. Stitch around, adding extra pieces as folds. Bias is wired to size. Bow trim at side. Brim is cut from a circle, placing collar towards the back. Wire outside edge; pull into a droop and cover with bias muslin. Add a wide satin bias bind.

Plate 18. Orange Panama Breton turned up a little all round; wide floral polyester material trim. Put 2'' (5 cm) folded bias piece around base of crown; a second bias piece for the top edge, thus giving a sweeping curve. Cut a third fairly wide piece, trim both edges and fold over centre. Tuck end under and place flower in position.

Plate 19. Light brown off-the-face Panama, petersham ribbon around brim. Swathe moiré together with ribbon and narrow petersham ribbon around crown. Use large bow for trim. The crown in this case was high enough, but a shallow crown can be extended with Sparterie to give the desired height.

Plate 24. Sequin whimsy. Make a small shape; wire and pad. Cover with stretch sequin material. Make tiger lily in same material with a little veiling for contrast. (Refer page 81.)

Plate 25. Pillbox variation. Use a ring block or just make a circle in Sparterie or Leno. Wire top and bottom in about ¾'' (18 mm), then turn. Cover with padding—foam or cotton wool. Block tip and wire around about ¾'' (18 mm) inside. Cover tip and circle with material. Push tip up from inside and stitch. Use two rows of petersham for trim and veiling. (Refer page 84.)

Plate 27. Pink Thai silk hats with straight brim and hand-tooled stiffened roses all round. Hat and cocktail hat base made of Sparterie or Leno covered with foam or padding. Bias edging. (Refer page 139.)

Plate 28. Silver/white wired whimsy. Use wire in the double piece over the head with cord only in the trim. Pull cord firmly and the curves will form naturally. (Refer page 111.)

Plate 29. Cocktail hats made with twelve folded bias pieces; cut 6¾'' wide × 7½'' long (170 mm × 190 mm), fold, and machine edges. Turn, but do not press. Gather at bottom. Make shape of Sparterie or Leno, cover with thin foam or cotton wool padding. Cut band 1'' (25 mm); cover with 3'' (7.5 mm) bias strip. (Refer page 81.)

Plate 31. Grey and white polyester beret. There are endless variations, using stitching, dints, and band widths. Tassel is made from fringing, bought by the metre. (Refer pages 37; 129.)

Millinery Manufacturers and Suppliers

S.A. Brown Pty Ltd (General Millinery Supplies)
Unit 5/52 Shepherd Street (off Broadway),
Chippendale, NSW 2008
Phone: (02) 699-7343 Fax (02) 698-3186.

Metchem Pty Ltd (formerly Stanfords) (Suppliers of Felt
Size, Straw Stiffener & Glue—Wholesale Quantities only).
21 Myrtle Street, Botany, NSW (Phone: 666-9320).

Bradford Potter Pty Ltd (Suppliers of flowers of all types)
608 Harris Street, Ultimo, NSW (Phone: 211-3277 &
211-3506).

Photios Bros Pty Ltd (Beading & Trimmings)
66 Druitt Street, Sydney, NSW (Phone: 267-1428).

Cyril J. Preston Pty Ltd
258 Flinders Lane, Melbourne, Vic, 3000
Phone (03) 654-7062

Distinctive Accessories
P.O. Box 128, Cleveland Qld 4183
Inquiries (07) 821-1506; Warehouse (07) 821-1570; Fax
(07) 266-5414

Paul Craig
14-15 D'Ablay St, London WIV 31P, UK

Jiffy Hat Steamer, Model J1
Jiffy Steamer Co.,
P.O. Box 869
Route 3, Union City TN 38261, USA

Miscellaneous

Micador A spray adhesive, multi-purpose, clear and fast
drying. For permanent and repositionable mounting.
Obtained from artist supply shops.
Scotch Magic Tape Withstands heat and steam, used for
finishing off ends of wire. Obtained from stationers.
Arbee Handicraft Spray An adhesive for all handicrafts,
colourless and fast drying.

Index